Dark Psychology and Manipulation:

How to Spot, Resist, and Reclaim Power from Manipulative Behaviour

Serena Haywood

Copyright © Serena Haywood, 2025 - All rights reserved.

The content contained within this book may not be reproduced, duplicated or transmitted without direct written permission from the author or the publisher.

Under no circumstances will any blame or legal responsibility be held against the publisher, or author, for any damages, reparation, or monetary loss due to the information contained within this book. Either directly or indirectly. You are responsible for your own choices, actions, and results.

Legal Notice:

This book is copyright protected. This book is only for personal use. You cannot amend, distribute, sell, use, quote or paraphrase any part, or the content within this book, without the consent of the author or publisher.

Disclaimer Notice:

Please note the information contained within this document is for educational and entertainment purposes only. All effort has been executed to present accurate, up to date, and reliable, complete information. No warranties of any kind are declared or implied. Readers acknowledge that the author is not engaging in the rendering of legal, financial, medical or professional advice. The content within this book has been derived from various sources. Please consult a licensed professional before attempting any techniques outlined in this book.

By reading this document, the reader agrees that under no circumstances is the author responsible for any losses, direct or indirect, which are incurred as a result of the use of the information contained within this document, including, but not limited to errors, omissions, or inaccuracies.

Contents

Introduction	5
Chapter 1: Foundations of Dark Psychology	7
Chapter 2: Understanding Manipulative People	14
Chapter 3: Manipulation Tactics Unveiled	18
Chapter 4: Emotional Manipulation Unraveled	30
Chapter 5: Psychological Manipulation in Relationships	34
Chapter 6: Workplace Manipulation Dynamics	38
Chapter 7: Digital Age Manipulation	43
Chapter 8: Defending Against Manipulation	49
Chapter 9: Setting Boundaries Effectively	53
Chapter 10: Healing and Moving Forward	58
Chapter 11: Real-Life Scenarios	62
Chapter 12: Empowerment through Knowledge	67
Chapter 13: Exploring Emotional Intelligence	71
Chapter 14: Identifying and Overcoming Pain Points	75
Chapter 15: Tools for Better Relationships	79
Chapter 16: Recognizing Manipulation in Media	82
Chapter 17: The Ethics of Influence	86
Chapter 18: Confront a Manipulator Without Losing Power (Bonus Chapter)	90
Chapter 19: Cultural Perspectives on Manipulation	99
Chapter 20: Building a Supportive Community	102
Chapter 21: Continuous Growth and Learning	107
Psychological Profile Test: Which Archetype Are You?	116
Your Free Downloadable PDF Resources	124
Support Resources	126
Glossary	129

Introduction

The air was sharp with a chill as I stepped into this networking event, hopeful and hungry for opportunity. Amidst the buzz of introductions and connections, I was deep in conversation with a magnetic entrepreneur - a sharp suit and a sharper smile. He spoke effortlessly, weaving a narrative where my skills perfectly aligned with his company's vision. By the night's end, I was buzzing, convinced I'd found my next big break in my late 20s. It wasn't until weeks later, when the promises faded into silence, that the truth hit me: I'd been expertly played with a masterful manipulation.

This disappointing experience and countless others sparked my curiosity and fascination with the hidden world of dark psychology and manipulation. Little did I know it was all around us in most of our experiences. These powerful forces shape our decisions, relationships, and lives in ways we often fail to recognize. From the boardroom to the bedroom, manipulation tactics are employed to influence, control, and exploit. But what exactly are dark psychology and manipulation?

Dark psychology refers to studying the human condition's darker aspects, such as selfishness, greed, and the desire for power. Conversely, manipulation covertly influences someone's thoughts, feelings, or behaviors for personal gain. Together, these concepts form a potent cocktail that can sway opinions, close deals, and even control entire groups of people without anybody involved even being aware.

In this book, I aim to empower you, the reader, with the knowledge and tools to recognize and defend against manipulation tactics. Whether you're a young woman navigating the complexities of relationships or a professional seeking to advance your career, understanding dark psychology and manipulation is essential for personal growth and improved interactions. It is crucial that you are equipped with all the information to make decisions that protect your true self, especially in this ever-changing world.

Throughout these pages, we'll explore the foundations of dark psychology, common manipulation techniques, psychological warfare, and the ethics of influence. You'll gain insights into how cult leaders control their followers, how advertisers persuade consumers, and how politicians sway public opinion. By the end of this book, you'll be equipped with the skills to spot manipulative tactics, build emotional resilience, and set healthy boundaries in your personal and professional life.

This book is more than just a passive reading experience. Each chapter includes exercises, reflection prompts, or interactive elements to help you engage more deeply with the material. You'll be able to analyze real-world examples, practice resistance techniques, and even craft your own ethical arguments.

It's important to note that this book is not a guide to becoming a master manipulator. While we'll explore the tactics used by those who seek to control others, our focus will be on empowering you to protect yourself and those around you from the adverse effects of manipulation. We'll also address common misconceptions about dark psychology, such as the idea that it's only relevant to criminal minds or that it's a foolproof way to get what you want.

As we embark on this journey together, I invite you to approach the material with an open mind and a willingness to challenge your assumptions. By understanding the darker aspects of human nature, we can shed light on the hidden influences that shape our world and take control of our own lives.

You'll find a 'Dark Psychology Quiz:' question at the end of each chapter in this book. These questions are designed to make you think about how you naturally react to influence, manipulation, and control - both when it's happening to you and when you might use it yourself. There are no right or wrong answers, just an opportunity to explore your instincts. Keep track of your responses as you go. By the end, you'll have a clearer picture of the role you tend to play when power and persuasion are at work.

So, are you ready to uncover the secrets of dark psychology and manipulation? Let's dive in and discover how to analyze anyone and influence human behavior, one page at a time.

Chapter 1: Foundations of Dark Psychology

In the heart of bustling city life, where the hum of ambition and the clangor of fast-paced routines reverberate, I found myself at a seemingly innocuous coffee shop meeting. The person sitting across from me, an acquaintance turned confidant, navigated the conversation with a precision that was almost surgical. Before I knew it, my thoughts, judgments, and even my planned actions seemed subtly directed by their words. The realization that I had been manipulated, not through overt demands but through nuanced suggestions, struck like a lightning bolt, prompting a profound curiosity about the forces that shape human behavior. This personal encounter is not an isolated incident, but a profound example of how dark psychology operates in the everyday world.

Dark psychology, a field that delves into the sinister aspects of human interactions, involves using psychological techniques to exploit, manipulate, and control others without their consent, often for personal gain or harm. Its roots stretch back to ancient times, evolving alongside human understanding of the mind as technological advancements provided new tools for influence. Historically, it has been employed by those seeking power, from cunning rulers to persuasive leaders, who understood that controlling thoughts and emotions could yield unparalleled power. Notable figures in psychology and sociology, from Robert Cialdini to Philip Zimbardo, have explored these dynamics, contributing to our understanding of how individuals can be subtly coerced or persuaded.

In contemporary society, dark psychology manifests in myriad ways, from the persuasive techniques in advertising on social media to political campaigns designed to sway public opinion by exploiting cognitive biases and emotional vulnerabilities. Recognizing these instances is crucial, as they reveal how pervasive manipulation can be and how they underscore the importance of understanding the mechanisms behind these behaviors.

The psychological theories underpinning dark psychology offer a fascinating yet unsettling glimpse into human nature. At its core lies the concept of the "dark triad," a trio of personality traits - narcissism, Machiavellianism, and psychopathy - characterized by manipulative and self-serving behaviors. Narcissism involves a grandiose sense of self-importance and a lack of empathy. At the same time, Machiavellianism is defined by strategic manipulation and deceit. Psychopathy, marked by impulsivity and a callous disregard for others, rounds out this triad. These traits are not confined to fictional villains; they can be found in everyday interactions, where individuals wield them to achieve their goals at the expense of others. Cognitive biases, such as confirmation bias and the halo effect, further complicate our perceptions, making it easier for manipulators to deceive and control. By exploiting these mental shortcuts, dark psychology practitioners can subtly alter beliefs and behaviors, often without the victim's awareness.

Despite its pervasive influence, dark psychology is not without its limitations and ethical considerations. While the field provides insight into the darker aspects of human behavior, it is essential to approach it with caution and a commitment to ethical practice. Misconceptions abound, such as the belief that understanding dark psychology equates to endorsing its use. The goal is to empower individuals with awareness and defense strategies against manipulation. Ethical considerations demand that we use this knowledge responsibly to protect ourselves and others rather than to exploit. Additionally, it is crucial to recognize that not all human interactions are deeply rooted in these darker dynamics; many are founded on empathy, trust, and genuine connection.

The relevance of dark psychology extends far beyond academic interest, impacting our daily lives in significant ways. In media and advertising, manipulative tactics are employed to shape consumer behavior, from the strategic placement of products to the creation of emotional narratives that drive purchasing decisions. These techniques often create a sense of urgency or fear of missing out, compelling consumers to act impulsively. Personal anecdotes from those who have experienced manipulation in relationships or workplaces reveal the subtle yet pervasive nature of these tactics. For instance, a colleague may use flattery and strategic alliances to climb the corporate ladder, leaving others feeling undermined or marginalized. Understanding these dynamics equips you to recognize them and empowers you to navigate them confidently and resiliently.

Identifying Manipulative Tactics

Reflect on a time when you felt influenced or pressured into making a decision that did not align with your values or desires. Consider the tactics and verbiage used and how they affected your thoughts and emotions. Jot down your observations here, focusing on how you can apply this awareness to future interactions. This exercise will help you develop a keen eye for manipulation, enhancing your ability to respond effectively and assertively.

Revelations of Dark Psychology Throughout Time

While psychology often focuses on understanding and improving mental wellbeing, dark psychology delves into the shadow side. Where persuasion turns into coercion, influence becomes manipulation, and trust is exploited for personal gain.

One of the most infamous examples of dark psychology in action is Charles Ponzi, the man behind the scheme that now bears his name. In the early 1920s, Ponzi promised investors extraordinary returns by exploiting international postage markets. His charisma, confidence, and carefully crafted promises lured people into parting with their money. But there was no real investment - just a cleverly disguised cycle of using new investors' money to pay earlier ones. By the time the scheme collapsed, Ponzi had swindled millions.

What made Ponzi so effective wasn't just the scam itself but his understanding of human psychology. He played on trust, greed, and urgency, convincing rational people to ignore red flags. This is the essence of dark psychology - not just manipulation but the ability to exploit cognitive biases and emotional vulnerabilities without the target even realizing it.

Ponzi and his infamous scheme were far from the first instance of dark psychology being wielded for personal or professional gain. Throughout history, influential figures have used manipulation to shape narratives and secure power. Let's delve into some striking examples from the past to give you a broader perspective on how these tactics have fueled propaganda and ambition.

Ancient History & Classical Era:

1. Sun Tzu's Psychological Warfare (5th Century BC)
   - THE ART OF WAR emphasized deception and mental manipulation as critical military tactics.
2. Cleopatra's Psychological Seduction (1st Century BC)
   - Cleopatra wielded charm and emotional manipulation to influence powerful leaders like Julius Caesar and Mark Antony.
3. Julius Caesar's Psychological Dominance (1st Century BC)
   - Caesar manipulated public perception through propaganda, solidifying his political power.

Medieval & Renaissance Period:

1. Machiavelli's Political Manipulation (16th Century)
   - The Prince advised leaders to use fear, deception, and manipulation to maintain control.
2. The Spanish Inquisition's Psychological Torture (1478 - 1834)
   - Fear, guilt, and mental torture were used to extract confessions and enforce religious conformity.
3. The Witch Hunts of Europe and America (15th - 18th Century)
   - Mass hysteria and emotional manipulation fueled accusations and executions, the most notorious being the Salem Witch Trials in colonial America.
4. Hernán Cortés and the Fall of the Aztec Empire (1519 - 1521)
   - Cortés exploited Aztec myths and alliances to dominate indigenous leaders psychologically.

Colonial & Enlightenment Era:

1. The East India Company's Divide-and-Conquer Strategy (1600s - 1800s)
   - Psychological manipulation fueled colonial expansion through the exploitation of local rivalries.

19th Century:
1. Napoleon Bonaparte's Cult of Personality (1800s)
   - Napoleon used propaganda and symbolic gestures, like crowning himself, to project authority.
2. The Psychological Exploitation Behind Barnum's Circus (1800s)
   - P.T. Barnum used cognitive biases, like curiosity gaps and confirmation bias, to attract audiences and celebrate hoaxes.

20th Century & Modern Era:

1. Rasputin's influence over the Russian Royal Family (Early 1900s)
   - Rasputin exploited fear and emotional vulnerability to manipulate the Tsarina and gain political sway.
2. Hitler and Nazi Propaganda (1920s - 1940s)
   - Hitler's regime used fear, groupthink, and propaganda to manipulate an entire nation.
3. The Rise of Mussolini and Fascist Propaganda (1920s - 1940s)
   - Mussolini controlled narratives through media and emotional appeals to maintain his dictatorship.

4. Charles Ponzi's Infamous Scheme (1920s)
   - Ponzi manipulated trust and greed to sustain his fraudulent investment scam.
5. The Twitter Bitcoin Scam (2020s)
   - Hackers used social engineering to manipulate users into transferring cryptocurrency.

The Power Dynamics in Human Interaction

Power dynamics are an inherent aspect of human relationships, often operating beneath the surface, weaving a complex web of interactions that dictate how individuals relate. Picture a team meeting at work where one person subtly dominates the conversation, steering the group's direction without overtly claiming authority. This individual manages to wield influence through confidence and strategic communication, effectively shifting the power balance in their favor. These subtle shifts, often unnoticed, illustrate the intricate dance of dominance and submission in social interactions. In friendships, families, and workplaces, power dynamics can manifest in various forms, whether through the authoritative presence of a dominant figure or the quiet acquiescence of a more submissive personality. Understanding these dynamics involves recognizing individuals' roles and their impact on relationships. By doing so, we can better navigate our social landscapes, ensuring that interactions remain equitable and respectful.

The wielding of authority and influence in group settings can often reshape the social fabric of an organization or community. Consider a scenario where a charismatic leader, much like the ones discussed in the previous section, uses their position to guide group decisions. Their authority, while sometimes necessary for direction, can overshadow individual contributions, leading to an environment where voices are stifled - much like in a business setting. This use of authority, if unchecked, can create an imbalance, fostering an atmosphere where people feel compelled to conform rather than contribute. Most of us have experienced a boss who works every hour of every day, setting an example that this is what they seek from their staff, leading to burnout. The psychological effect of such dynamics can be profound, as individuals may internalize feelings of inadequacy or powerlessness. In these settings, the balance of power often hinges on the ability to influence others, whether through persuasion, coercion, or manipulation. Recognizing the signs of power imbalance is crucial, as it allows individuals to address these dynamics constructively, ensuring everyone has an equal opportunity to participate and contribute.

Manipulation and control tactics often alter power dynamics, subtly shifting the balance to favor one individual over another. Gaslighting, for instance, is a particularly insidious tool used to create power imbalances by making someone question their reality. Think of a partner who consistently denies or distorts facts about their poor or abusive behavior to make the other feel confused or insecure. This tactic undermines confidence and establishes a dependency on the manipulator to validate reality. Similarly, coercive persuasion in personal and professional environments can manifest through pressure tactics, guilt-tripping, or emotional manipulation, effectively stripping away an individual's autonomy and agency. By breaking down these manipulative tactics, we can better understand how they operate and learn to recognize them in our own interactions, paving the way for more equitable relationships.

The psychological impact of power imbalances can be far-reaching, profoundly affecting mental and emotional wellbeing. When subjected to manipulation, individuals may experience heightened anxiety and stress, unsure of their footing in relationships where control is uneven. This stress can infiltrate all aspects of life, leading to long-term effects on self-esteem and trust. A person who consistently feels overshadowed or manipulated may begin to doubt their worth or capability, leading to a cycle of self-doubt that is difficult to break. Trust, once eroded, can be challenging to rebuild, and the emotional toll of power imbalances can linger long after the dynamics have shifted. Understanding these effects highlights the importance of addressing power imbalances head-on, where addressing them upfront is ideal, fostering environments where individuals feel valued and respected.

Recognizing and responding to power shifts in interactions is essential for maintaining balanced relationships. One effective strategy is learning to assert boundaries confidently. Individuals can protect their autonomy and prevent undue influence by clearly communicating personal limits. For instance, if a colleague repeatedly takes credit for your ideas, it is crucial to address the behavior directly, reinforcing your contributions and establishing clear expectations for future interactions. Also, developing effective communication strategies can empower individuals to navigate power-imbalanced situations with poise. This might involve practicing active listening, ensuring that all parties feel heard and respected, or employing conflict resolution techniques to address disagreements constructively. By honing these skills, we can create healthier dynamics in our personal and professional lives, fostering relationships built on mutual respect and understanding.

Exploring power dynamics reveals the subtle yet profound ways influence and control shape our interactions. By understanding the mechanisms at play, we can equip ourselves with the tools to recognize and address imbalances, ensuring that our relationships are grounded in equity and respect. Through awareness and intentionality, we can create environments where everyone feels empowered to contribute and thrive, free from the constraints of manipulation and control.

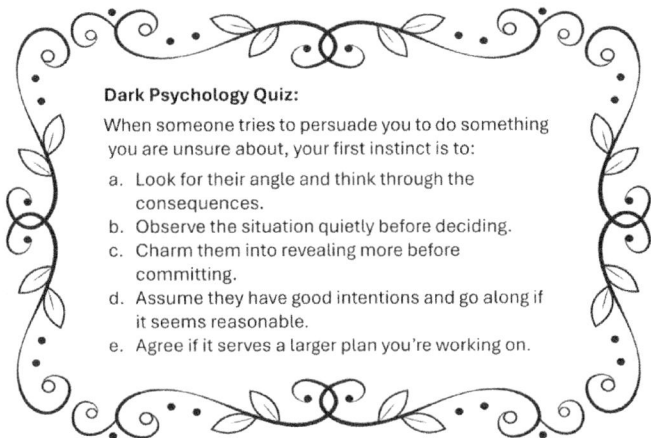

Dark Psychology Quiz:

When someone tries to persuade you to do something you are unsure about, your first instinct is to:

a. Look for their angle and think through the consequences.
b. Observe the situation quietly before deciding.
c. Charm them into revealing more before committing.
d. Assume they have good intentions and go along if it seems reasonable.
e. Agree if it serves a larger plan you're working on.

Chapter 2: Understanding Manipulative People

Manipulators often possess an uncanny ability to enchant and persuade, making them appear trustworthy and genuine. Their charm is a powerful tool for deception, allowing them to influence and control those around them without raising suspicion. Yet, this allure is often a facade, masking their true intentions and lack of genuine empathy.

At the heart of manipulative behavior lies a profound absence of empathy and an emotional coldness that enables individuals to exploit others without remorse. This lack of empathy allows manipulators to prioritize their needs above all else, often at the expense of those who trust them. They may view relationships as transactions where the primary goal is to maximize personal gain. This emotional detachment can be particularly damaging, as it leaves victims feeling used and devalued, questioning their worth and the authenticity of their connections. Understanding these core traits is crucial in recognizing manipulators who often hide behind a veneer of kindness and concern.

Manipulative individuals exhibit specific behavioral patterns that can help you identify them in various situations. Frequent lying and deceitfulness are hallmarks of manipulation, as these individuals often rely on falsehoods to create an illusion of truth. They may fabricate stories or alter facts to suit their narrative, leaving others bewildered and unsure of reality. Inconsistent behavior and mood swings further complicate matters, as manipulators often shift their demeanor to maintain control. One moment, they may appear nurturing and supportive; the next, they become distant and critical. This unpredictability creates confusion, making it difficult for others to anticipate their actions or intentions, ultimately fostering a sense of dependency.

Communication styles are pivotal in a manipulator's arsenal, allowing them to exert influence through verbal and non-verbal cues. Persuasive language, often laced with flattery, is a common tactic to win trust and gain favor. Manipulators may lavish compliments, making you feel valued and admired, only to later wield this praise as a tool for control. Their body language can be equally telling, as they may use intimidation or coercion to assert dominance. A subtle change in posture, eye contact, or even a dismissive gesture can communicate power and authority, steering interactions in their favor. Recognizing these cues is vital in identifying manipulation, as they often reveal the true dynamics. Learning how not to rise to these behaviors is also essential.

Various tools and methods can be employed to effectively assess manipulative traits, providing practical insights into interpersonal dynamics. One such tool is the Dark Triad Personality Test, which evaluates the presence of narcissism, Machiavellianism, and psychopathy - traits commonly associated with manipulative behavior. This assessment offers a glimpse into the personality characteristics that drive manipulation, allowing for a deeper understanding of underlying motivations. Additionally, red-flag checklists can be invaluable in evaluating personal interactions, highlighting behaviors that may indicate manipulation. These checklists include signs such as excessive charm, frequent lying, and a pattern of exploiting others, serving as a guide for identifying potential manipulators in your life.

Personal Exercise: Recognizing Manipulative Traits

Take a moment to reflect on a recent interaction where you felt uneasy or uncertain. Consider the person's behavior, communication style, and any inconsistencies you noticed. Use a journal to document these observations, focusing on traits that align with manipulative behavior. This exercise can help sharpen your awareness and enhance your ability to recognize manipulation in the future.

Understanding the traits and patterns of manipulators is an empowering step toward protecting yourself and those you care about. You can navigate relationships with greater confidence and assertiveness by identifying these characteristics. This knowledge equips you to defend against manipulation and fosters healthier, more authentic connections. Through awareness and vigilance, you can ensure that your interactions are grounded in trust and mutual respect, free from the shadows of deceit and control.

Understanding the Manipulator's Mindset

To truly comprehend manipulative behavior, one must first explore the psychological motivations that drive it. Manipulators often harbor an insatiable desire for control and dominance, seeking to orchestrate the dynamics of their relationships and environments to suit their needs. This craving for power can stem from a deep-seated fear of vulnerability and insecurity. For many, manipulation becomes a way to shield themselves from perceived threats, whether they are emotional, social, or professional. Controlling the narrative and dictating the terms of engagement, manipulators create a facade of strength that masks their underlying fragility. This need for control often manifests subtly, such as dictating the flow of conversation or steering interactions toward outcomes that benefit them most.

Cognitive distortions, a common feature in the manipulator's mindset, further complicate these motivations. These exaggerated or irrational thought patterns skew reality to fit the individual's narrative. Rationalization is a frequent tactic, allowing manipulators to justify their harmful actions as necessary or justifiable. They might dismiss their deceitful behavior as a means to an end or convince themselves that their actions are in the best interest of their victims. This reality distortion enables them to act without guilt as they view their actions through a self-serving lens. Projection is another common cognitive distortion in which manipulators attribute their negative traits or intentions to others. They deflect accountability and maintain their image of superiority by shifting the focus away from themselves. This blame-shifting tactic protects their ego and destabilizes their victims, who may begin to question their perceptions and judgments.

Emotional detachment is crucial in a manipulator's toolkit, allowing them to exploit others without remorse. This detachment can manifest as alexithymia, a condition characterized by an inability to identify and express emotions. Individuals with alexithymia often struggle to empathize with others, viewing emotions as foreign or irrelevant. This lack of emotional connection makes it easier for them to manipulate without guilt, as they remain unaffected by the emotional fallout of their actions. Emotional numbing serves as another coping mechanism, where manipulators consciously or unconsciously suppress their feelings to avoid vulnerability. By numbing their emotions, they create a barrier between themselves and their actions, enabling them to engage in manipulative behavior without internal conflict. This detachment can be particularly damaging to their targets, who may feel isolated and confused by the manipulator's apparent lack of genuine emotion.

Interacting with manipulators requires a strategic approach that prioritizes safety and mental wellbeing. One effective strategy is setting firm boundaries and maintaining a safe distance. Clearly defined boundaries act as a protective barrier, preventing manipulators from overstepping and exerting undue influence. Limiting personal disclosures or keeping conversations focused on neutral topics can deter attempts to exploit vulnerabilities.

In a romantic relationship, clearly defined boundaries can protect against emotional manipulation.

For example, imagine Lisa and Mark dating for a few months. Mark often pries into Lisa's past, especially about her insecurities and past traumas, using this information later to guilt-trip or control her. To protect herself, Lisa sets a boundary: she chooses not to disclose deeply personal experiences until trust is established. Instead, she steers conversations toward neutral topics like shared interests, hobbies, or future goals. When Mark presses for more details about her past, Lisa calmly but firmly says, "I prefer to keep some things private until I feel ready to share." By maintaining this boundary, she reduces the risk of emotional exploitation while also gauging Mark's respect for her limits.

This approach prevents manipulators from using sensitive information as leverage, ensuring that emotional intimacy grows on mutual trust rather than coercion.

Communicating these boundaries assertively ensures the manipulator understands acceptable behavior limits. Additionally, maintaining a safe distance, whether physical or emotional, can reduce the manipulator's ability to control the situation. This might involve minimizing contact or disengaging from uncomfortable or invasive conversations.

Identifying safe exit strategies is another crucial component of coping with manipulative individuals. Recognizing when a situation is becoming harmful and knowing when to walk away can prevent further manipulation. This may involve having a predetermined excuse to leave a conversation or social setting, providing an immediate escape route when necessary. Having supportive allies - friends or colleagues who understand the dynamics and can provide assistance or validation is also helpful. In professional settings, documenting interactions with manipulators can serve as a safeguard, ensuring there is a record of events if needed. This documentation can also provide clarity and perspective, helping to discern patterns of manipulation that may not be immediately apparent. Recording these behaviors and their instances in professional settings can also assist with formal complaints to safeguard your mental wellbeing.

Understanding the manipulator's mindset equips us to recognize and respond to manipulation and empowers us to protect our emotional wellbeing. The next chapter will delve into specific manipulation techniques, offering practical strategies to counteract these tactics in everyday life.

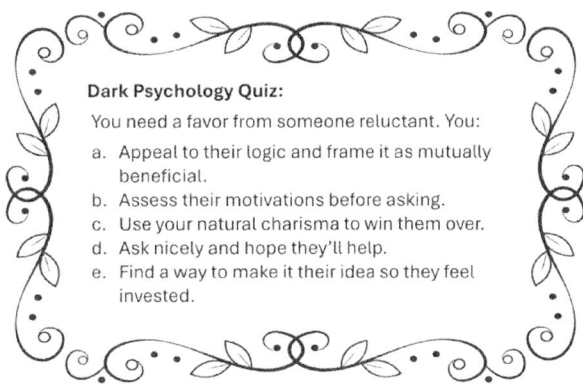

Dark Psychology Quiz:
You need a favor from someone reluctant. You:
a. Appeal to their logic and frame it as mutually beneficial.
b. Assess their motivations before asking.
c. Use your natural charisma to win them over.
d. Ask nicely and hope they'll help.
e. Find a way to make it their idea so they feel invested.

Chapter 3: Manipulation Tactics Unveiled

The day seems calm until an unexpected email from a colleague arrives, subtly suggesting errors in your recent project. Confused, you open the attachment only to find discrepancies in the files you were sure you had perfected the night before. As you stare at the screen, an unsettling feeling creeps in - doubt clouds your mind. This scenario, familiar to many, may be an example of gaslighting. This manipulation tactic distorts reality and undermines your confidence.

Gaslighting, a term rooted in the 1938 British play "Gas Light" and its subsequent film adaptations, is a psychological manipulation tactic that aims to seed doubt in the victim's mind. The gaslighter, often a single deceitful individual, employs this strategy to make the victim question their perceptions, memories, and even sanity. The term gained prominence from the play, where a husband manipulates his wife into believing she is losing her grip on reality by altering their environment and denying his actions, much like Roald Dahl's 'The Twits.' This manipulation often involves reality distortion, where the gaslighter skillfully bends truth and falsifies events to maintain control. It's not merely a tool of fiction; it's a devastatingly effective method utilized in real life to exert power over others, often leading victims to depend on the gaslighter for a sense of reality.

Gaslighters employ various techniques to maintain their pretense and keep victims in a state of confusion. One common method is the strategic use of denial and contradiction. For instance, if you confront a gaslighter about a broken promise, they might insist they never made it, leaving you bewildered. This tactic erodes your confidence in your memory and perceptions, making you second-guess your grasp of reality. Manipulation of evidence or past events is another insidious technique. A gaslighter may alter details or present false information to make you question your recollections. They might, for example, alter messages or emails to support their version of events, further confusing your sense of truth. Feigned concern and false reassurance add another layer to their manipulation. A gaslighter might express worry for your wellbeing, suggesting that stress or external factors affect your memory, thereby positioning themselves as caring while undermining your self-trust.

The psychological effects of gaslighting can be profoundly damaging, often leading to long-term impacts on a victim's mental health. As the gaslighter's tactics take hold, victims may develop self-doubt and the habit of second-guessing themselves. This erosion of self-trust is a hallmark of gaslighting, leaving individuals feeling insecure and disoriented. Over time, the persistent questioning of one's reality can heighten anxiety and foster feelings of alienation, as victims may begin to isolate themselves, doubting their experiences and fearing judgment from others. The power of gaslighting lies in its ability to fracture an individual's sense of self, making it challenging to discern truth from manipulation. This internal chaos can lead to increased stress, depression, and a sense of powerlessness, trapping victims in a cycle of uncertainty and dependency on the gaslighter for validation and clarity.

I've personally suffered at the hands of a master gaslighter, and it took me years to overcome the anxiety and helplessness they caused me. Reaching out to friends to clarify my strength of character was a lifesaver for me, as it helped me eliminate the feelings of self-doubt, confusion, and worthlessness planted in my mind.

Gaslighting thrives on isolation and uncertainty, making it crucial to reconnect with reality through trusted relationships. I found that journaling my experiences also helped, allowing me to see patterns in their manipulation and remind myself that I wasn't imagining things. Seeking therapy provided me with concrete strategies to rebuild my confidence, and learning about dark psychology gave me the tools to recognize manipulation before it could take hold again.

Recovery wasn't instant; it was a process of unlearning false narratives, reclaiming my independence, and setting firm emotional boundaries moving forward. But over time, I regained my sense of self, and now, I no longer question my reality based on someone else's distortions. If you're in this, know that clarity, strength, and healing are possible - and you are not alone.

Recognizing and combating gaslighting requires vigilance and proactive strategies to safeguard your mental health and reality. One practical approach is to keep a written record of interactions with the suspected gaslighter. Documenting conversations, events, and discrepancies can provide clarity and a tangible reference point to counteract manipulated narratives. This practice helps reaffirm your memory and serves as evidence if the need arises to confront the gaslighter or seek external assistance. Seeking validation from trusted sources is another crucial strategy.

Sharing your experiences with friends, family, or a mental health professional can offer a new perspective and support, helping to ground your perceptions in reality. Trusted individuals can offer objective insights and affirmations, countering the isolation and confusion that gaslighting often induces. It's also essential to reaffirm your perception and memory. Engaging in self-reflection and trusting your instincts can bolster your confidence, allowing you to assert your reality despite attempts to distort it. Mindfulness practices and grounding exercises can enhance your awareness and emotional resilience, empowering you to navigate gaslighting with greater clarity and strength. Stay strong.

Strengthening Reality

Take a few moments to reflect on a situation in which you felt your reality was questioned or distorted. Please write down the details as you remember them, focusing on your feelings and perceptions at the time. Compare your account with any written records or external validations you may have. Reflect on how this exercise reinforces your confidence in your memory and helps you identify potential gaslighting tactics. This practice can fortify your sense of reality and equip you with the confidence to trust your perceptions.

Love Bombing

This tactic serves a more sinister purpose beneath the surface: to manipulate emotions and establish control. Love bombing operates on the psychology of overwhelming affection, where the recipient is showered with intense flattery, lavish gifts, and constant communication. This barrage of affection creates an emotional high, leaving you feeling unique, adored, and deeply connected to the person who seems to have entered your life like a dream come true. Yet, the critical difference between genuine affection and manipulation lies in the intent. Genuine affection grows steadily, respecting boundaries and mutual interests. At the same time, love bombing aims to create dependency, drawing you into the manipulator's sphere of influence.

The tactic of love bombing unfolds in distinct stages, each designed to deepen emotional entanglement and dependency. Initially, you might experience an intense flood of flattery and praise, with your new partner making you feel like the most important person in their world. Every interaction is filled with compliments and affirmations, creating euphoria that can be both exhilarating and addictive. As the relationship progresses, milestones that typically take time to reach are suddenly rushed. Discussions about moving in together, meeting family members, or even marriage proposals might come sooner than expected. This rapid escalation cements the bond, making it harder to step back or question the pace without feeling guilty or ungrateful. However, a shift often occurs once the initial stages set the hook. The once lavish attention may wane, replaced by subtle forms of withdrawal and punishment. If you begin to assert independence or question the relationship's dynamics, you might find affection withheld or subtle criticisms creeping in.

This withdrawal serves as a control mechanism, ensuring that you remain compliant and eager to return to the relationship's initial intoxicating phase.

The emotional consequences of love bombing can be profound, leaving lasting impacts that ripple through subsequent interactions and relationships. Feelings of confusion and emotional whiplash can emerge as the initial euphoria fades. You're left wondering how something that began so beautifully could become fraught with tension and unease. Distinguishing genuine affection from manipulation becomes increasingly challenging as the lines between love and control blur. This confusion fosters a sense of dependency, where you might question your perceptions and seek to recapture the initial intensity that defined the relationship's early days. This cycle can erode self-esteem and lead to emotional vulnerability, making it difficult to trust your instincts and creating a reliance on external validation from the manipulator.

Building emotional resilience and establishing healthy relationship boundaries are crucial steps in preventing and recovering from the effects of love bombing. Setting emotional boundaries early in a relationship can safeguard against manipulation, ensuring that both parties move comfortably and respect each other's autonomy. Communicating openly about your needs and limits is essential, as well as resisting pressure to accelerate the relationship. Seeking objective advice from trusted friends or counselors can provide valuable perspective and support, helping you evaluate the relationship more clearly. An external viewpoint can highlight potential red flags that might be difficult to see within the relationship. Another vital strategy is developing a strong sense of self-worth independent of external validation. Cultivating self-confidence and a robust support network reinforces your ability to maintain healthy boundaries and recognize genuine affection. This inner strength is a buffer against manipulation, empowering you to prioritize your wellbeing and make choices that align with your values.

Recall the Rush

Think back to when someone showered you with attention, affection, and grand gestures very early in the relationship - more than felt natural.

Think of the following:
- How soon did they express deep feelings?
- Did they talk about fate, soulmates, or moving fast (living together, marriage, future plans) within the first few weeks?

- Did their level of attention make you feel almost overwhelmed, but you brushed it off as romantic?

Please write down the specific things they said or did that felt too good to be true. Did they constantly buy expensive gifts, text, or immediately make you feel like the center of their world? After the initial intensity, did you notice a sudden change in their behavior? Looking back now, how real do those over-the-top declarations of love feel?

Create two lists:
- What healthy love looks like (steady growth, respect for boundaries, space to breathe)
- What love bombing looks like (excessive attention, fast-tracking intimacy, overwhelming communication)

Keep these lists somewhere visible. Next time someone sweeps in with over-the-top affection too soon, pause - trust that real connection builds over time. Healthy relationships don't need to sprint to feel secure.

DARVO: The Ultimate Manipulation Shield

When confronted with wrongdoing, most people take responsibility or attempt to explain their actions. But some go further; they deflect, attack, and twist the narrative until the accuser becomes the accused. This tactic, known as DARVO (Deny, Attack, Reverse Victim and Offender), is a psychological manipulation strategy commonly used by abusers, narcissists, and anyone unwilling to face accountability. It silences victims, makes them question their reality, and shifts the power dynamic entirely.

The first stage of DARVO is denial. The manipulator outright refuses to acknowledge wrongdoing, no matter how much evidence exists. "That never happened," they might say, or "You're imagining things." Doing this, they plant doubt in the victim's mind, forcing them to second-guess their own perception. If denial alone doesn't work, the second stage kicks in: attack. Instead of engaging with the accusation, they go on the offensive, belittling or gaslighting the victim into submission. "You're always looking for problems," they might snap. "You're so insecure." The goal is to force the victim onto the defensive, turning the conversation away from the manipulator's actions and toward the victim's supposed faults.

The final stage of DARVO is the role reversal. At this point, the manipulator flips the script entirely, making themselves the victim and the actual victim the aggressor. "I can't believe you're treating me this way," they might exclaim, their voice full of indignation. "After everything I've done for you, now I'm the one being attacked?" This tactic is particularly insidious because it preys on the victim's empathy. A person who initially sought justice may now find themselves apologizing, desperate to fix a situation that wasn't their fault in the first place.

Take, for example, Sophie and Jake. Sophie discovers messages proving Jake has lied to her about meeting his ex. When she confronts him, Jake immediately denies it. "That's not true!" he insists, even though Sophie has already seen the proof. When she pushes further, he pivots to attack mode. "You're so jealous and controlling," he spits. "You always overreact to things." Trying to stay rational, Sophie points out that trust is vital in their relationship. That's when Jake delivers the final blow: "You don't trust me at all! You're making me feel terrible when I've done nothing wrong!" By the end of the conversation, Sophie - who had every right to feel betrayed - is left feeling guilty, while Jake walks away unscathed.

DARVO is not exclusive to personal relationships. It appears in workplaces where toxic managers turn complaints against employees who speak up. It thrives in politics, where public figures use it to dodge scandals. It's used in legal battles, where abusers paint themselves as victims to escape consequences. The strength of this tactic lies in its ability to confuse, exhaust, and demoralize the victim until they either drop the issue or accept a false reality.

How to Defend Against DARVO

- Stay Calm & Stick to Facts - Don't get pulled into emotional arguments. Keep the focus on the issue at hand.
- Recognize It in Action - If someone denies, attacks, and flips the narrative, it's DARVO.
- Don't Fall for the Guilt Trip - Remind yourself that their actions are the issue, not your reaction.
- Set Boundaries & Walk Away - If they refuse accountability, disengage. You don't owe them a debate.
- Document Everything - If this happens at work or in a legal situation, keep records of manipulative behaviors.

DARVO is gaslighting on steroids - a manipulator's way of dodging responsibility while making you feel like the bad guy. The key is to see it for what it is, refuse to engage in their narrative, and stand firm in your truth.

Personal Exercise: Flip The Script

Think of a time when you confronted someone about a real issue, only to defend yourself instead. Write down the original problem you brought up. Then, list how the other person denied, attacked, and reversed the roles. How did they shift the conversation?

Stay focused on your original concern and refuse to be baited into defending yourself. Use a firm, neutral statement like, "We're not talking about me right now. We're talking about what you did."

Projection: The Mirror of Manipulation

One of the most frustrating and insidious manipulation tactics is projection. In this defense mechanism, a person accuses someone else of the very behavior they are guilty of. Rather than admit their faults, they shift the blame onto their victim, forcing them into a defensive position. This psychological trick deflects responsibility and confuses and destabilizes the person on the receiving end, making them question their behavior.

At its core, projection allows the manipulator to avoid accountability. Instead of confronting their actions, they project their insecurities, misdeeds, or desires onto their partner, friend, or colleague. This tactic is particularly effective because it triggers self-doubt in the victim, making them more likely to defend themselves rather than examine the manipulator's behavior. The more someone fights to prove their innocence, the less they focus on the actual issue - the manipulator's wrongdoing.

Consider a classic example: a cheating partner who constantly accuses their significant other of being unfaithful. At first, the accusations seem baseless, even paranoid. The accused partner may reassure them, offering transparency - sharing phone messages, schedules, or locations - believing that proving their innocence will ease the tension. But over time, the accusations don't stop. They escalate. The cheating partner becomes more aggressive, more suspicious, and more invasive. The irony is that their accusations often mirror their actions - they are the ones being unfaithful.

By projecting their guilt onto their partner, they accomplish two things:
1. They deflect suspicion away from themselves. By keeping their partner on the defensive, they create a smokescreen that ensures their infidelity remains hidden.
2. They gain control over their partner. Constant

accusations make the innocent party doubt themselves, making them more anxious, apologetic, and eager to prove their loyalty.

This is not just a tactic used in relationships; projection exists in every sphere of life - friendships, workplaces, and even politics. A workplace manipulator who steals ideas might accuse a colleague of trying to take credit for their work. A controlling friend who constantly talks behind people's backs might warn you about "fake friends" and insist others are gossiping about you. On a larger scale, authoritarian leaders throughout history have used projection to frame their opponents as "corrupt" while secretly engaging in the very corruption they claim to condemn.

The effects of projection can be psychologically draining. Victims often internalize the accusations, wondering if they've somehow done something wrong. They may second-guess their reality, spending more energy defending themselves than analyzing the manipulator's actions. Over time, this can lead to a complete shift in power, where the victim becomes emotionally exhausted, hyper-vigilant, and desperate for approval.

How to Defend Against Projection

The key to resisting projection is awareness. If someone is constantly accusing you of something that seems entirely out of character, take a step back and ask:
- Is this something I've actually done?
- Or is this a reflection of their behavior?

Refusing to engage in endless defense is also critical. Instead of justifying yourself, turn the focus back onto the accuser:
- "Why do you keep accusing me of this?"
- "Strangely, you bring this up so often - why does this seem to bother you so much?"

If you suspect projection in a relationship, watch for patterns. Does the accuser's behavior match the things they accuse you of? Are they suspicious without cause? If so, recognize that their accusations may have more to do with their guilt than anything you've done.

Projection is a form of psychological warfare - it shifts blame, distorts reality, and wears down a person's confidence. But its power crumbles once you learn to spot it for what it is. The moment you stop accepting the blame for someone else's actions, you break the cycle of manipulation.

Mirror, Mirror on The Wall

Have you ever been accused of something you never did - only to realize later that the accuser was guilty? Think back to that situation. What behaviors made you suspect they were projecting? How did it affect your confidence? Jot down some thoughts on this.

Instead of defending yourself, shift the focus back to them: "Interestingly, you keep bringing this up. Is there something you need to tell me about your own life?"

Normalizing Toxic Behavior: When Manipulation Becomes "Normal"

One of the most subtle yet damaging manipulation tactics is normalizing toxic behavior - convincing the victim that what they're experiencing isn't manipulation at all but simply the way things are. Over time, this creates an altered sense of reality, where the victim comes to accept mistreatment as a normal part of relationships.

This tactic often starts small. A partner, friend, or family member may dismiss concerns when the victim points out unhealthy patterns. If the victim says, "I feel like you're being controlling," the manipulator may respond with: "All relationships have ups and downs; stop making a big deal out of nothing." When repeated over time, the victim internalizes that their expectations for respect and fairness are unreasonable.

A classic example of this is seen in emotionally abusive relationships. Suppose a partner constantly insults, belittles, or guilt-trips their significant other. When confronted, they may say, "This is just how couples argue," or, "If you can't handle it, maybe you're too sensitive." By making the victim feel overly emotional, demanding, or complex, the manipulator reinforces the idea that the victim's boundaries are the problem - not the abuse itself. Over time, this form of manipulation can cause learned helplessness. The victim stops resisting in this state because they believe this is just how relationships work. This makes it much harder to recognize mistreatment, let alone leave.

How to Defend Against Toxic Behavior

- Trust your gut. Don't let someone convince you otherwise if something feels wrong, demeaning, or unfair.
- Compare healthy vs. unhealthy dynamics. Ask yourself: Would I tolerate this behavior if a friend were going through it?
- Listen to outside perspectives. Abusers often isolate their victims; talking to trusted friends, family, or a therapist can help break the illusion of normalcy.

Weed Out The Toxicity

When have you been told, "All relationships are like this" or "This is just how things work" after expressing discomfort?

Compare that situation to a healthy example from a past relationship, a friend's experience, or even a book/movie with positive dynamics. What differences stand out? Please write down the comparisons so you can remember them.

If a behavior feels wrong, trust yourself. Tell the manipulator, "Just because you're used to this doesn't mean I have to accept it." And then leave and free yourself.

Lying & Deception: Controlling Through Falsehoods

Manipulators often use outright lies or half-truths to control their victims. These falsehoods create a false reality, keeping the victim misinformed, confused, and dependent on the manipulator for "truth." Lying in manipulative relationships can take many forms. Some lies are small and frequent, like lying about where they were, who they were with, or what they said earlier. Other lies, such as hiding financial issues, past relationships, or secret behaviors, are much more significant. A person who wants control will distort reality just enough to ensure the victim never has a complete picture of the truth.

For example, imagine a partner lying about their financial status. They might tell their significant other, "I'm just bad with money," when in reality, they are deliberately hiding debt, gambling, or financial fraud. By withholding key details, they ensure that their partner cannot make informed decisions about their shared finances, future, or trust in the relationship.

Similarly, a manipulator may lie about their whereabouts to cover up cheating or double lives. They may double down on their deception if confronted, making the victim feel paranoid for even asking. Over time, the victim may stop trusting their perception, leading them to doubt what is real and what is not. This breakdown of reality makes deception so dangerous - it erodes a victim's ability to trust their instincts.

How to Defend Against Lying & Deception

- Look for patterns. One or two small lies might be mistakes, but consistent dishonesty is manipulation.
- Fact-check when possible. If someone's words don't match their actions, believe actions over words.
- Set a firm boundary with dishonesty. Make it clear that

trust is non-negotiable and repeated lying has consequences.

Discovering a chronic liar

Think of a time you caught someone in a lie that affected your trust. How did they react when confronted? Did they double down or try to gaslight you? List the warning signs that seemed minor at the time but, in hindsight, pointed to dishonesty. Jot down some thoughts.

If someone has a pattern of lying, trust actions over words. Set boundaries around honesty, and if they continue, walk away.

Exploiting Vulnerabilities: Using Past Trauma as a Weapon

Perhaps one of the cruelest forms of manipulation is exploiting a person's deepest wounds, insecurities, or traumas against them. This tactic is designed to keep the victim dependent, ashamed, and trapped in the relationship.

A manipulator doesn't just notice vulnerabilities - they weaponize them. If a person has a history of abandonment, insecurity, or low self-esteem, the manipulator will use it to control their thoughts and behavior. For instance, a partner might say, "No one else would love you after everything you've been through." This preys on the victim's fear of being unlovable, making them less likely to leave, even if the relationship is toxic.

This manipulation is widespread when the victim has a history of past abuse. The abuser reframes reality, making the victim feel undeserving of better treatment. In extreme cases, this can lead to trauma bonding, where the victim becomes emotionally attached to the person harming them.

This tactic takes a different form in friendships or workplaces. A toxic boss might prey on an employee's insecurities, saying things like, "You're lucky to even have this job, considering your lack of experience." Similarly, a friend might constantly remind you of your past mistakes to keep you in a submissive role. By exploiting vulnerabilities, the manipulator ensures the victim never feels secure enough to leave or advocate for themselves.

How to Defend Against Exploiting Vulnerabilities:

- Recognize emotional blackmail. If someone frequently brings up your past mistakes, traumas, or fears to keep you small, they control you.

- Know your worth. Your past does not define you, and your vulnerabilities are not excuses for mistreatment.
- Distance yourself. If someone constantly reminds you of your weaknesses rather than empowering you, they do not have your best interests at heart.

These tactics are designed to break down a person's sense of reality, self-worth, and independence. The key to overcoming them is awareness. When you start recognizing these behaviors for what they are, their power diminishes. No one deserves to live under constant manipulation, and the moment you realize you have the right to set boundaries, demand honesty, and walk away from toxic situations, you take back control.

Consider how these tactics intertwine with other manipulation strategies. Understanding these dynamics helps you navigate relationships with clarity and confidence, equipping you to identify manipulative patterns and prioritize healthy interactions. Next, we'll delve into the broader context of psychological warfare, examining how these tactics fit into wider strategies of influence and control.

Reframing

Has someone ever weaponized your past mistakes, childhood trauma, or insecurities to make you feel unworthy? Identify a statement they made that deeply hurt you, write it down, and remember it so it can't be used on you in the same way again. Then, reframe it from your perspective - instead of "No one else would love me," say, "My experiences make me stronger, not unlovable." When someone uses your past against you, shut it down: "My past is not up for discussion. If you can't respect that, we don't need to continue this conversation."

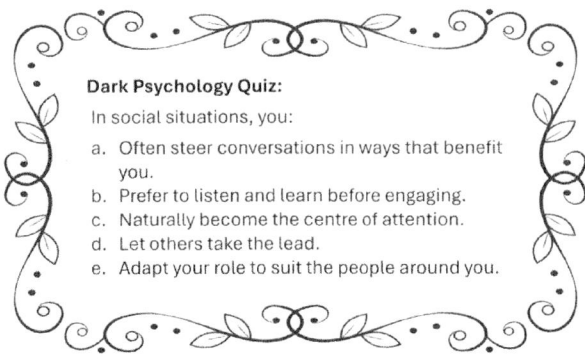

Dark Psychology Quiz:
In social situations, you:
a. Often steer conversations in ways that benefit you.
b. Prefer to listen and learn before engaging.
c. Naturally become the centre of attention.
d. Let others take the lead.
e. Adapt your role to suit the people around you.

Chapter 4: Emotional Manipulation Unraveled

Emotional blackmail is a calculated tactic employed by manipulators to control and coerce their victims, leveraging the powerful triad of fear, obligation, and guilt (FOG) to achieve their ends. This concept, popularized by psychotherapist Susan Forward, often unfolds within close personal relationships, where trust and vulnerability are most pronounced. Picture a relationship where every decision is scrutinized, and the fear of disappointment or retribution shadows every choice. Emotional blackmailers thrive in these environments, weaving their web through subtle threats and calculated guilt trips, making you feel trapped and compelled to comply.

The psychological mechanism behind emotional blackmail hinges on the induction of guilt, a powerful emotion that can cloud judgment and enforce compliance. Guilt, when wielded strategically, becomes a tool for manipulators to ensure that you act in accordance with their desires. They might frame their needs or sacrifices to make you feel obligated to reciprocate, even if it comes at a personal cost. Typical scenarios include parents who expect unwavering loyalty from their children, partners who demand constant reassurance, or friends who subtly manipulate situations to prioritize their needs. In each case, the underlying message is clear: failure to comply will result in negative consequences, whether emotional, relational, or reputational.

Emotional blackmailers are adept at employing specific techniques that amplify feelings of guilt and fear, making their victims feel responsible for outcomes. One such technique is the threat of negative consequences. This might manifest as a partner threatening to leave or withdraw affection if their demands aren't met, creating a fear of loss that compels compliance. Another tactic is emotional withdrawal as punishment. A friend might suddenly become distant or cold if you fail to meet their expectations, leaving you scrambling to mend the perceived rift. This withdrawal acts as a silent reprimand, reinforcing your perceived failure. Exaggerating personal sacrifices to invoke guilt is another powerful tool in the emotional blackmailer's arsenal. They might remind you of all they've done for you, painting a picture of selfless devotion that makes you feel indebted and eager to repay the perceived debt. In each scenario, the manipulator's goal is to create a sense of obligation that overrides your needs and desires, ensuring their demands take precedence.

The psychological impact of emotional blackmail on victims can be profound and far-reaching, often manifesting in chronic feelings of inadequacy and self-blame. When faced with constant demands and guilt induction, you might question your worth and capabilities, doubting your ability to make sound decisions without external validation. This erosion of self-esteem can lead to increased anxiety and stress within relationships as you become hyper-aware of the manipulator's potential reactions and adjust your behavior accordingly to avoid conflict. Decision paralysis is another common outcome, where the fear of repercussions stifles your ability to make choices confidently. You may find yourself second-guessing every decision, worried about how it might be perceived or whether it will lead to emotional fallout. This constant state of vigilance can be emotionally draining, leaving you feeling powerless and trapped in a cycle of compliance and guilt.

To resist emotional blackmail and reclaim your autonomy, it's crucial to establish and communicate clear personal boundaries. These boundaries serve as a protective barrier, ensuring your needs and values are respected. Begin by identifying non-negotiable aspects of your relationships, such as mutual respect and open communication, and communicate these expectations confidently. Practicing assertive communication techniques is another effective strategy. Use "I" statements to express your feelings and needs without assigning blame, which can help defuse potential conflicts and assert your standpoint. For instance, saying, "I feel uncomfortable when decisions are made without my input," clearly conveys your perspective without escalating tension. Seeking support networks for validation and perspective is also essential. Surround yourself with individuals who understand your situation and can provide objective insights and encouragement. This support can bolster your confidence and offer a fresh perspective on the dynamics at play, helping you navigate the complexities of emotional blackmail with resilience and clarity.

Establishing Boundaries

Take a moment to reflect on a relationship where you feel your boundaries have been compromised. Identify specific instances where you felt pressured or guilted into compliance. In a journal, write down what boundaries you would like to establish and how you plan to communicate them. Consider potential challenges and how you might overcome them. This exercise will help you clarify your boundaries and prepare you to assert them confidently in future interactions.

Weaponizing Empathy: The Costs of Caring

Empathy, a quality that bridges gaps and fosters genuine understanding, can also be cleverly manipulated by those who recognize its power. At its core, empathy involves the ability to share and understand the feelings of another, forming connections that are both profound and nurturing. However, individuals who see empathy as a tool for manipulation rather than mutual support can exploit this same capacity for connection. They draw a fine line, distinguishing between authentic concern and calculated exploitation. Genuine empathy is a two-way street characterized by reciprocal care and mutual respect.

In contrast, manipulative empathy is one-sided, designed to extract emotional resources from others while giving little in return. The manipulator uses empathy to create a veneer of vulnerability, ensnaring their target in a web of obligation and guilt. This exploitation is a subtle art, often disguised as a genuine need, making it challenging to discern and even harder to resist.

Manipulators adept at weaponizing empathy often employ various tactics to achieve their goals. One common strategy is fabricating or exaggerating victimhood. By presenting themselves as victims of circumstance, they elicit sympathy and support from those around them. This tactic involves detailed stories of hardship and adversity, often accompanied by visible displays of emotion that reinforce their narrative. The manipulator aims to draw upon the listener's compassion, creating a dynamic where the empathetic individual feels compelled to offer assistance or support. Selective vulnerability is another powerful tool in their arsenal. By strategically revealing personal struggles or insecurities, manipulators create an illusion of openness that fosters trust. This selective disclosure is calculated and designed to elicit sympathy without exposing the manipulator's true intentions. Lastly, playing on others' inherent desire to help is a tactic that leverages the natural inclination to assist those in need. By positioning themselves as someone who requires aid, manipulators exploit the goodwill of empathetic individuals, often leading them to prioritize the manipulator's needs over their own.

The consequences for empathetic individuals who fall prey to these tactics can be severe, often leading to a cycle of emotional exhaustion and compassion fatigue. As they continually extend support and understanding to those who exploit their empathy, they may be depleted, struggling to maintain their energy and emotional wellbeing. This constant giving, without the balance of reciprocal support, can quickly lead to burnout, leaving empathetic individuals feeling drained and overwhelmed. The difficulty in maintaining personal boundaries compounds the emotional toll of such manipulation. When one's natural inclination is to care and support, setting limits can feel counterintuitive, erasing personal space and autonomy. Over time, this can foster resentment and frustration, as the empathetic individual realizes they are being taken advantage of yet feels powerless to change the dynamic.

It is crucial to build resilience and foster healthy empathy to protect oneself from the pitfalls of empathy manipulation. Developing emotional awareness and self-regulation is the first step in this process. By cultivating a keen understanding of one's emotions and triggers, you can better identify when your empathy is being manipulated and respond accordingly. This awareness empowers you to manage your emotional responses, ensuring that your compassion is directed appropriately. Learning to discern genuine need from manipulation is another vital skill. By critically evaluating the intentions and consistency of those who seek your support, you can distinguish between authentic requests for help and manipulative ploys. This discernment allows you to allocate your emotional resources wisely, preserving your energy for truly reciprocal and supportive relationships. Encouraging reciprocal relationships that foster mutual support is the final piece of the puzzle. By surrounding yourself with individuals who respect and value your empathy, you create an environment where care and support are balanced and sustainable. This mutual exchange enhances your wellbeing and strengthens the bonds of friendship and trust, ensuring that your empathy is a source of strength rather than vulnerability.

The journey through emotional manipulation is fraught with challenges. Armed with knowledge and awareness, you can navigate these waters with confidence. By understanding the tactics of empathy exploitation and building the skills to resist manipulation, you empower yourself to maintain healthy, fulfilling relationships. As we move forward, we'll explore the psychological warfare tactics that further illuminate the complex dance of influence and control.

When you recognise the signs early and respond with clear boundaries, you shift from being reactive to being in charge of your emotional space.

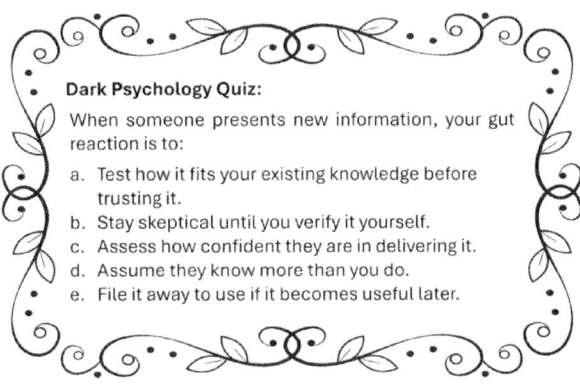

Dark Psychology Quiz:
When someone presents new information, your gut reaction is to:
a. Test how it fits your existing knowledge before trusting it.
b. Stay skeptical until you verify it yourself.
c. Assess how confident they are in delivering it.
d. Assume they know more than you do.
e. File it away to use if it becomes useful later.

Chapter 5: Psychological Manipulation in Relationships

In the early days of a romantic relationship, everything often feels like a dream. You're swept off your feet, and emotions run high. Yet, beneath the surface of this seeming bliss, subtle signs may hint at a darker reality. These early warning signs of manipulation are frequently overlooked due to the intoxicating nature of love and initial attraction. You might find yourself dismissing behaviors that, in retrospect, are glaring red flags. Excessive jealousy and possessiveness can initially appear as flattering gestures of care and attention. However, when a partner constantly questions your whereabouts or becomes unreasonably possessive, it signals a desire to control rather than cherish. Such jealousy is not a testament to love but an indication of insecurity and a need for dominance.

Attempts to isolate you from friends and family are another early sign of manipulation that can be mistaken for devotion. A partner might express disdain for your social circle or subtly discourage you from spending time with loved ones, framing it as a need for exclusivity. Yet, this tactic removes you from your support system, making you more dependent on them for emotional fulfillment. Over time, this isolation can erode your sense of self and increase your vulnerability to further manipulation. Moreover, frequent blaming or shaming language is a clear red flag. This behavior manifests as a partner constantly criticizing or belittling you, often under the guise of jokes or sarcasm. While it may start subtly, it gradually chips away at your self-worth, leaving you questioning your value and capabilities.

These patterns of control and dominance don't emerge overnight; they evolve, gaining strength as the relationship progresses. Initially, you might not notice the gradual erosion of personal autonomy. It begins with small concessions, like altering your schedule to accommodate their needs or preferences. Soon, you find yourself prioritizing their desires over your own, sacrificing your independence bit by bit. Monitoring of personal communications and activities often follows. A partner might insist on knowing who you're texting or demand access to your social media accounts, all in the name of transparency. This behavior, however, is a breach of trust and a clear indication of control, as they seek to monitor and influence your interactions with the outside world.

The impact of these manipulative behaviors on your self-esteem can be devastating. Constant criticism or undermining of your achievements diminishes your sense of self-worth. When every success is met with skepticism or downplayed, you begin to doubt your abilities and question the validity of your accomplishments. Emotional withdrawal, particularly as a response to boundary-setting, is a common tactic. When you attempt to assert your independence or express discomfort, they might respond with silence or distance, making you feel guilty for disrupting the status quo. This withdrawal serves as a punishment, reinforcing that compliance is the only path to harmony in the relationship.

Recognizing these red flags early and taking proactive steps can prevent further entrenchment in a manipulative dynamic. Open communication about boundaries and expectations is crucial. Clearly articulating your needs and limits establishes a foundation of mutual respect and understanding. It is essential to communicate these boundaries assertively, ensuring that both parties understand the parameters of acceptable behavior. Seeking external perspectives from trusted friends or counselors can provide valuable insights and guidance. An external viewpoint can highlight potential red flags that might be difficult to see within the relationship. Consulting with those who have your best interests at heart offers clarity and helps you discern unhealthy patterns.

Setting and upholding boundaries is vital to maintaining personal space and independence. This might involve preserving your social connections, pursuing personal goals, or dedicating time to self-care. Independence is a right and a necessity, allowing you to retain your identity and autonomy within the relationship. By nurturing your interests and maintaining a strong sense of self, you fortify your resilience against manipulation and foster a dynamic prioritizing equality and mutual respect.

Identifying Your Boundaries

Consider your current or past relationships and reflect on moments when your boundaries were challenged. Write down specific instances and how they made you feel. In another column, list the boundaries you wish to establish moving forward. Consider how you can communicate these boundaries effectively. This exercise will help you identify areas where you must assert yourself and reinforce your autonomy. Write these down to reflect on.

Navigating Emotional Triggers and Manipulation

Emotional triggers are like invisible wires that run through our lives, ready to spark at the slightest touch. They are deeply personal, often rooted in past experiences that have left a lasting imprint on our emotional landscape. Understanding these triggers is crucial because they can significantly impact how we respond to situations, especially in relationships. For instance, a seemingly innocuous comment might send you spiraling into self-doubt or anger simply because it taps into an unresolved issue from your past. Identifying these triggers requires introspection and honesty. Reflect on moments when you've reacted more intensely than the situation warranted. Consider what past events might be influencing your current emotions. By acknowledging these patterns, you gain insight into your vulnerabilities, which is the first step toward managing them more effectively.

Manipulators are skilled at exploiting these emotional triggers, often using them to control and influence behavior. They know precisely what buttons to push to provoke a desired reaction, creating a cycle of dependency and emotional turmoil. For example, they might deliberately provoke guilt or shame during conflicts, making you feel responsible for their feelings or actions. This tactic shifts the focus away from their behavior and onto your perceived shortcomings, leaving you feeling inadequate. Similarly, manipulators might play on your fears of abandonment or rejection, suggesting that any attempt to assert independence will lead to loss or isolation. This creates a powerful emotional hook, binding you to them through fear and uncertainty. The result is a relationship dynamic where your emotional responses are manipulated to serve their needs, often at the expense of your wellbeing.

Developing emotional awareness is key to recognizing when manipulation is occurring. By cultivating this awareness, you empower yourself to break free from the cycle of manipulation. One effective technique is grounding, which involves anchoring yourself in the present moment to gain clarity and perspective. When you feel emotionally triggered, take a moment to pause, breathe deeply, and focus on your immediate surroundings. This practice can help you distance yourself from the emotional intensity and respond more calmly and rationally. Self-reflection is another valuable tool. Regularly journaling about your emotional responses and patterns can reveal insights into your triggers and how they are being used against you. Over time, this practice builds self-awareness, enabling you to identify manipulation and respond confidently.

Building emotional resilience is equally vital in responding to manipulation with strength and clarity. Mindfulness practices like meditation or yoga can enhance your ability to regulate emotions and maintain composure under pressure. These techniques foster a sense of inner peace and stability, reducing the likelihood of being swayed by external influences. Establishing a support system for emotional validation is also crucial. Surround yourself with people who understand and respect your emotional needs, providing a safe space for open communication and support. This network can offer reassurance and perspective, helping you navigate challenging situations more resiliently.

Additionally, engaging in self-care practices is vital for maintaining mental health. Prioritize activities that nourish your wellbeing, whether it's taking a relaxing bath, engaging in a creative hobby, or spending time in nature. Investing in self-care strengthens your emotional foundation, making it harder for manipulators to destabilize you.

In understanding and managing emotional triggers, you gain the tools to protect yourself from manipulation and foster healthier relationships. Recognizing how past experiences shape your reactions allows you to approach interactions with greater insight and intentionality. By building emotional resilience, you empower yourself to respond to challenges with clarity and strength, ensuring that your relationships are grounded in mutual respect and authenticity. This awareness is a defense against manipulation and a pathway to deeper self-understanding and growth. As we move forward, we will explore the broader context of psychological manipulation and its impact on various aspects of life, equipping you with the knowledge to navigate these dynamics with confidence and integrity.

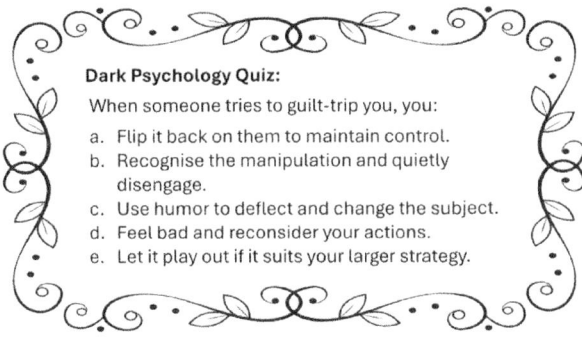

Dark Psychology Quiz:

When someone tries to guilt-trip you, you:

a. Flip it back on them to maintain control.
b. Recognise the manipulation and quietly disengage.
c. Use humor to deflect and change the subject.
d. Feel bad and reconsider your actions.
e. Let it play out if it suits your larger strategy.

Chapter 6: Workplace Manipulation Dynamics

Office politics, an invisible yet palpable force, shapes your daily environment. A complex web of relationships and power dynamics influences career progression, job satisfaction, and workplace culture. At its core, office politics involves individuals' strategic actions to influence others and gain position beyond usual processes. This can manifest in forming alliances, seeking endorsements, and leveraging networks to climb the corporate ladder. For many women, office politics is negatively associated with stress and reduced job satisfaction. Yet, understanding this intricate dance is crucial for not only surviving but thriving in professional settings.

Within every organization, informal power structures exist, subtly dictating how decisions are made and who holds influence. These structures often operate alongside formal hierarchies, creating a dual system of authority that can be both empowering and exclusionary. Those who navigate these waters successfully usually do so by building alliances and networks that bolster their standing. These alliances are not limited to hierarchical relationships; they can include peers, mentors, and even subordinates who advocate for one another. Networking, therefore, becomes a vital skill, enabling individuals to forge connections that transcend departmental boundaries and foster collaborative opportunities. However, it's essential to approach these relationships with authenticity and mutual respect, ensuring that alliances are rooted in genuine support rather than mere transactional exchanges.

Certain manipulative tactics are commonly employed in office politics, often with subtlety that belies their impact. One such tactic is information hoarding and selective disclosure, where individuals control the flow of information to maintain an advantage. By withholding critical details or selectively sharing knowledge, they position themselves as indispensable while leaving others in the dark. This manipulation can lead to unpreparedness or failure among colleagues, undermining team cohesion. Another tactic is undermining colleagues through gossip or exclusion. Whispered rumors and deliberate exclusion from meetings or projects can damage reputations and create a hostile work environment. This behavior fosters division and distrust, eroding the collaborative spirit necessary for effective teamwork. Strategic flattery to gain favor with superiors is another common practice, where individuals use insincere praise to curry favor and secure preferential treatment. While this tactic may yield short-term advantages, it often breeds resentment among peers, who see through the façade and question the individual's sincerity.

The effects of office politics on workplace morale are significant, impacting both individual wellbeing and organizational productivity. The stress of navigating these dynamics can lead to burnout and decreased job satisfaction, as employees feel undervalued or sidelined. Trust among team members is also eroded when political maneuvering takes precedence over genuine collaboration. This erosion of trust creates an atmosphere of suspicion, where individuals hesitate to share ideas or support one another, fearing ulterior motives. As trust dwindles, team collaboration and cooperation suffer, hindering innovation and progress. The broader implications for team dynamics are profound, as a fractured workforce struggles to achieve common goals and maintain a harmonious work environment.

It didn't happen all at once - it crept in slowly like a door being quietly closed behind my back. I was leading a major project I'd been heavily involved in from the start. It was the kind of work I was proud to put my name on, something I'd invested time, energy, and creativity into.

Then, without warning, meetings started happening - without me. Decisions were being made, plans were being shifted, and conversations I should have been part of were moving forward behind closed doors. The worst moment came when I discovered the client was being handed over my project, and I hadn't even been asked for input. I wasn't just being excluded - I was being erased.

The silence was the hardest part. No one came to me directly. There were no conversations about concerns, no performance reviews, and no explanation at all. It was just an eerie, professional ghosting - like I was there, but not really. My name stayed on some emails, but my voice had been completely removed from the process.

I felt insecure, blindsided, and honestly, a little humiliated. I knew I needed clarity, so I went to HR for advice. To their credit, they took it seriously. The closing out - the quiet, deliberate isolation - was wrong, and it was addressed professionally.

The experience left me with a hard-earned lesson: being locked out isn't just a communication failure - it's a form of control. Sometimes, the only way to reclaim your power is to step out of the silence and demand to be heard.

To navigate office politics effectively while maintaining integrity, consider adopting strategies emphasizing transparency and ethical decision-making. Building genuine relationships based on mutual respect is paramount. These relationships, grounded in trust and open communication, provide a foundation for constructive dialogue and collaborative problem-solving. Strong communication skills and assertiveness further enhance your ability to convey ideas and advocate for your interests. You foster an environment where diverse viewpoints are valued and integrated by articulating your perspective and actively listening to others.

Practicing transparency in your interactions reinforces ethical decision-making and diminishes the negative effects of office politics. Being open about your intentions and actions builds credibility and fosters trust among colleagues. Additionally, aligning with positive influencers within the company can provide guidance and support as you navigate complex dynamics. These individuals, who focus on gaining trust and admiration rather than exerting power, can serve as mentors and role models. By observing their approach and learning from their experiences, you can develop your political acumen while staying true to your values. Embracing these strategies enables you to advance your career with integrity, contributing positively to your organization's culture and success.

Office Politics Reflection Exercise

Reflect on a recent situation where office politics played a role. Consider the dynamics at play, the individuals involved, and the outcome. Write about how you navigated the problem and what you learned. Identify any tactics used and how they affected your approach. This exercise will help you develop greater awareness of political dynamics and refine your strategies for future encounters.

Dealing with Narcissistic Bosses and Colleagues

Navigating the workplace can feel like walking through a maze, especially when you encounter narcissistic individuals who complicate the path. Recognizing narcissistic traits in bosses and colleagues is crucial for maintaining your equilibrium. These individuals often exhibit grandiosity, an inflated sense of self-importance that permeates their interactions. Picture a manager who constantly boasts about their past achievements, overshadowing the contributions of their team. This behavior is not just about confidence; it signals a more profound need to assert superiority. Alongside this, a lack of empathy is a hallmark of narcissistic personalities. They may dismiss your concerns or overlook the team's needs, prioritizing their desires above all else. This disregard can manifest in decisions that seem self-serving, with little consideration for how they affect others. Moreover, narcissists crave constant admiration and validation, seeking praise and acknowledgment to bolster their self-image. You might notice a colleague fishing for compliments or subtly maneuvering conversations to highlight their accomplishments. This need for validation often drives their interactions and can create a challenging dynamic where others feel unappreciated or ignored.

Working with narcissistic individuals presents unique challenges affecting team dynamics and individual performance. One of the most significant hurdles is the frequent criticism and unrealistic expectations they impose on others. A narcissistic boss might set unattainable goals, pushing their team to the brink with little regard for the consequences. This pressure can lead to burnout as employees strive to meet impossible demands. Additionally, narcissists often struggle to accept feedback or criticism, perceiving it as a threat to their carefully constructed self-image. When faced with constructive criticism, they may react defensively or dismissively, making it challenging to address issues or improve processes. Another common behavior is the tendency to take credit for others' work. You might find a narcissistic colleague presenting your ideas as their own or receiving accolades for a team effort without acknowledging the contributions of others. This behavior undermines morale and can create a toxic environment where collaboration is stifled and resentment brews.

Despite these challenges, you can employ practical coping mechanisms and strategies to protect your mental wellbeing and professional integrity. One of the most effective strategies is setting clear boundaries and managing expectations. Clearly communicate your limits and stand firm when they are challenged. This might involve asserting your availability for additional tasks or reinforcing your role and responsibilities within the team. Maintaining a paper trail by documenting interactions can also be invaluable. Keep records of meetings, decisions, and communications, noting key details and outcomes. This documentation serves as a reference point and provides evidence should disputes arise. In addition to these strategies, regular self-care and stress management is crucial. Prioritize activities that replenish your energy and support your mental health, whether through exercise, meditation, or hobbies that bring you joy. By nurturing your wellbeing, you can build resilience against the stressors associated with narcissistic personalities.

Building a supportive network within the workplace is another vital aspect of counteracting the influence of narcissistic individuals. Seek mentorship and guidance from experienced colleagues who can offer insights and advice on navigating complex dynamics. These mentors can provide perspective, helping you see beyond the immediate challenges and focus on long-term goals. Collaborating with peers to foster a positive work environment is equally important. Building strong relationships with your colleagues creates a sense of camaraderie and mutual support that can counteract the negativity of a narcissistic presence. To address concerns and seek additional support, utilize company resources, such as HR or employee wellness assistance programs. These resources can offer guidance on conflict resolution, stress management, and personal development, empowering you to navigate workplace challenges with confidence and grace.

In the realm of workplace dynamics, dealing with narcissistic personalities requires a blend of awareness, strategy, and support. By recognizing the traits and challenges associated with narcissistic individuals, you can implement effective coping mechanisms and build a robust support network. These strategies protect your wellbeing and enhance your ability to thrive professionally. As we explore further, the focus will shift to understanding broader psychological manipulation tactics, providing you with even greater tools to navigate and succeed in complex environments.

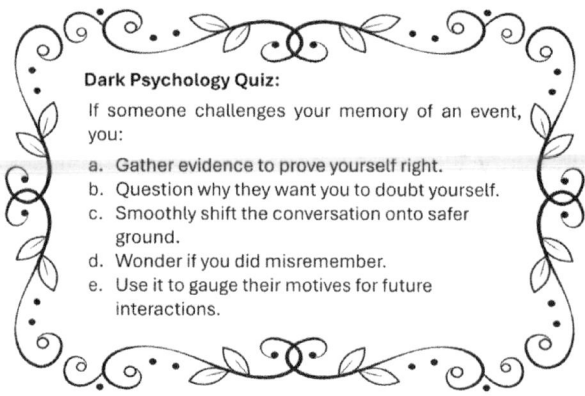

Dark Psychology Quiz:

If someone challenges your memory of an event, you:

a. Gather evidence to prove yourself right.
b. Question why they want you to doubt yourself.
c. Smoothly shift the conversation onto safer ground.
d. Wonder if you did misremember.
e. Use it to gauge their motives for future interactions.

Chapter 7: Digital Age Manipulation

Picture yourself scrolling through your social media feed on a lazy Sunday morning. Your thumb flicks through a cascade of images and headlines, each vying for a moment of your attention. A post catches your eye - a friend has shared a link with a shocking headline, and you feel a surge of curiosity mixed with disbelief. As you click through, you realize the article is more sensational than factual, leaving you questioning its intent. This scenario is familiar in the digital age, where social media platforms wield immense power to shape perceptions and influence behavior.

With their sleek interfaces and engaging content, social media platforms are masterfully designed to capture and hold your attention. Behind this engagement lies a complex web of algorithms - rules and computations that curate what you see based on your interactions and interests. These algorithms do more than personalize your feed; they create echo chambers where your existing beliefs are reinforced and opposing perspectives are quietly filtered out. As you engage with content that aligns with your views, the algorithm learns, tailoring your feed to mirror your preferences. This phenomenon, known as confirmation bias, can skew your perceptions, making it difficult to discern fact from fiction. While these algorithms connect you with like-minded individuals and new interests, they can also foster social media addiction and raise privacy concerns, as your online behavior is meticulously tracked and analyzed.

The impact of viral trends and challenges on user behavior is profound. These trends can sweep through social media like wildfire, prompting collective participation and influencing cultural norms. Whether it's a viral dance challenge or a hashtag campaign, these trends often capitalize on the fear of missing out (FOMO), compelling you to join in for fear of being left behind. The rapid spread of such content shapes public opinion and blurs the line between genuine engagement and contrived participation. As these trends gain momentum, they can influence consumer behavior, driving demand for products or ideas that seem universally accepted. The algorithms that drive social media platforms play a pivotal role in amplifying these trends, ensuring they reach a vast audience and perpetuate their influence.

Manipulative content strategies abound on social media, designed to provoke strong emotional reactions and sway perceptions. With their sensational promises and tantalizing questions, clickbait headlines lure you into clicking on articles that often fall short of their claims. These headlines prey on your emotions, whether it's curiosity, anger, or fear, compelling you to engage with content that may not be credible. Memes and viral content further complicate the landscape as they spread misinformation with alarming speed. A cleverly crafted meme can convey a misleading message, masquerading as humor or satire yet carrying the power to shape beliefs. The visual nature of memes makes them particularly potent, as they bypass critical analysis and appeal directly to your emotions.

The influence of influencers and sponsored content on social media cannot be underestimated. With their curated personas and relatable content, influencers wield significant sway over consumer behavior. They operate in a space where the line between personal endorsements and paid promotions is often blurred, creating a dynamic where trust and relatability are leveraged to drive sales. Consumers, particularly those under 45, are drawn to influencer posts as a primary method for discovering new products. The psychology of trust plays a central role here, as influencers build rapport with their audience, positioning themselves as genuine and authentic. This trust is a powerful tool, enabling influencers to subtly manipulate perceptions and decisions, often without the audience realizing the extent of the influence.

As you navigate the labyrinth of social media, developing a discerning eye is crucial for critical consumption. Verifying the source and credibility of information is the first step in this process. Before accepting content at face value, consider its origin and its motivations. Fact-checking tools and resources are invaluable allies in this endeavor. Open-source intelligence (OSINT) tools, such as InVID for verifying videos and Google Image Search for reverse-image analysis, can help you evaluate content validity. Comprehensive fact-checking sites like Snopes offer insights into rumors and fake news, guiding you toward informed conclusions. Engaging with diverse perspectives is another essential strategy. You broaden your understanding and cultivate a balanced perspective by seeking viewpoints that challenge your biases. This approach not only deepens your insight but also equips you to navigate the complexities of social media with confidence and clarity.

TikTok's Control Over You

Social media platforms have long been accused of manipulating their users. Still, TikTok has elevated this to an art form, blending sophisticated algorithms with the fundamental principles of dark psychology to create one of the most addictive digital experiences ever designed. TikTok doesn't just entertain - it hijacks the brain's reward system, exploiting our emotional vulnerabilities, cognitive biases, and primal need for social validation to keep us endlessly scrolling.

At the heart of TikTok's addictive power is the infinite scroll, a design choice that triggers the exact psychological mechanisms as slot machines. Each swipe delivers new, unpredictable content, flooding the brain with tiny dopamine hits. These quick surges of pleasure fuel a constant craving for the next reward, keeping users glued to their screens, hoping the following video will be even better than the last.

The platform's infamous For You Page (FYP) takes this further by rapidly learning each user's preferences. Within minutes, TikTok can map your emotional triggers, serving you a highly personalized feed tailored to your fears, desires, insecurities, and sense of humor. This level of personalization feels intimate, even uncanny, giving the illusion that the app understands you better than your closest friends. That illusion creates an emotional attachment to the feed itself, blurring the line between curiosity and compulsion.

Adding to this psychological pull is TikTok's mastery of emotional contrast. A viral dance might follow a heartbreaking personal story, then a shocking news clip, and finally, a relatable skit. This emotional whiplash keeps the brain in a state of heightened arousal, unable to predict or fully process what's coming next. The constant shifts in tone heighten engagement, ensuring that even if you're emotionally exhausted, your curiosity keeps you swiping.

For creators, TikTok offers a different kind of manipulation: the promise of viral fame and instant validation. Every like, comment, and share is a micro-reward, tapping into the universal human desire for social approval. Even for passive viewers, the comment sections act like mini communities, pulling users deeper into conversations, debates, and in-jokes. This creates a powerful fear of missing out (FOMO), making leaving the app feel like social exile.

The short format itself is also part of the trap. Each video feels like a harmless investment of a few seconds, making it easy to justify watching "just one more." But TikTok's seamless, uninterrupted flow distorts the passage of time, leading to hours lost before the brain even registers the extent of the distraction. This time distortion is another example of dark psychological design, exploiting the mind's inability to accurately measure small, repeated actions.

Most disturbingly, TikTok's algorithm can exploit users' vulnerabilities, serving content that aligns with insecurities, anxieties, and unresolved traumas. Whether it's content about body image, toxic relationships, or wealth comparison, TikTok preys on emotional wounds, triggering negative feelings that the app then soothes with the next wave of dopamine-rich distractions. This cycle is a classic manipulation tactic disguised as personalized entertainment.

In essence, TikTok is a perfect storm of psychological exploitation, blending dopamine loops, emotional manipulation, social engineering, and cognitive distortion into a platform that doesn't just capture attention - it takes emotional and psychological hostages. The more you understand how it works, the more you can begin to take back control, one mindful swipe at a time.

Social Media Content Checklist

Use this checklist to critically evaluate social media content before accepting it as fact:
- Verify the source: Is it reputable and credible?
- Check for sensational language: Are headlines designed to provoke emotion?
- Use fact-checking tools: Have you cross-referenced the information?
- Consider the author's intent: What might be their motivation?
- Seek diverse perspectives: Have you considered opposing viewpoints?

This list will help you approach social media content critically, ensuring that your online experience is informed and intentional.

Cyberbullying and Online Emotional Blackmail

As you navigate your digital life, it's crucial to understand the insidious nature of cyberbullying and online emotional blackmail. These tactics have become alarmingly prevalent in the digital realm, affecting individuals across all walks of life. Cyberbullying involves aggressive acts carried out through electronic communication, often characterized by anonymity, which emboldens perpetrators to act without fear of immediate consequences. This anonymity can lead to behaviors such as doxxing, where personal information is maliciously exposed, and trolling, where individuals deliberately provoke or harass others to elicit emotional responses. Both tactics aim to intimidate and control, leveraging the expansive reach of the internet to maximize impact.

The psychological toll of cyberbullying and online emotional blackmail can be profound. Victims often experience heightened anxiety and depression due to the relentless nature of online harassment. The digital sphere, once a source of connection and information, becomes a battleground fraught with stress and fear. This constant barrage of negativity can lead to digital PTSD, a relatively new term recognizing the mental health repercussions of sustained online abuse. Victims may relive distressing interactions repeatedly, leading to nightmares, avoidance behaviors, and a pervasive sense of fear. The emotional scars left by such experiences can take a significant toll on one's mental wellbeing, affecting all aspects of life, from personal relationships to professional endeavors.

Recognizing the signs of cyberbullying and online emotional blackmail is the first step in combating these issues. Sometimes, harassment might not be overt; it can manifest through subtle, passive-aggressive comments or exclusionary tactics that undermine confidence and self-worth. Watch for persistent negative interactions or messages that make you uneasy. Most social media platforms offer tools for reporting abuse designed to protect users from harmful content and interactions. Familiarize yourself with these tools, which can be powerful allies in maintaining a safe online environment. Reporting abusive behavior protects you and contributes to a safer community by holding perpetrators accountable.

Building resilience against online abuse requires a proactive approach. Developing a personal online code of conduct can be an empowering step. This involves setting clear guidelines for engaging with others online, interacting positively, and disengaging from toxic exchanges. Another effective strategy is engaging in digital detoxes. Taking regular breaks from social media and online platforms can help reset your mental state, reduce stress, and improve overall wellbeing. During these breaks, focus on activities that nourish your mind and body, such as reading, exercising, or spending time with loved ones. This balance between online and offline life is essential for maintaining mental health.

Online support groups and forums can also offer valuable connections and shared experiences, fostering a sense of community and solidarity. Joining these groups allows you to connect with others who may have faced similar challenges, providing a space for empathy, advice, and support. These communities can remind you that you are not alone, reinforcing your resilience against online negativity. Sharing your experiences and learning from others can empower you to navigate the digital world with greater confidence and assurance.

Resource List: Tools for Online Safety

- Block and Report Features: Familiarize yourself with platform-specific tools to block and report abusive users.
- Privacy Settings: Regularly review your privacy settings to control who can view and interact with your content.

- Unfollow Accounts: You are not at liberty to continue to consume content that harms you or manipulates you to feel a certain way - unfollow accounts that do this.
- Support Hotlines: Keep a list of mental health support hotlines available for immediate assistance.

As we explore the complexities of digital manipulation, it's essential to remain vigilant and informed. Understanding the mechanics of cyberbullying and emotional blackmail equips you with the tools to protect yourself and others. By fostering supportive communities and prioritizing mental health, you can navigate the digital landscape with confidence and resilience. In the next chapter, we will delve deeper into strategies for recognizing and overcoming manipulation in various aspects of life, empowering you to build a more secure and fulfilling existence.

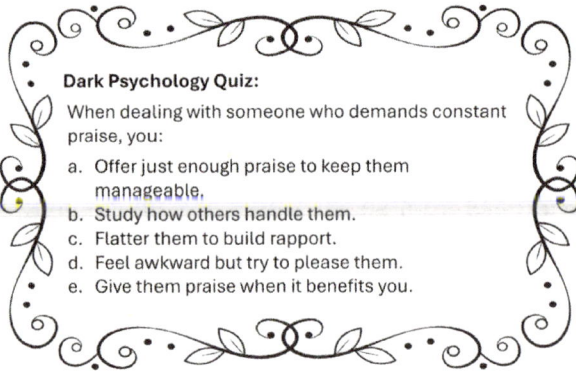

Dark Psychology Quiz:

When dealing with someone who demands constant praise, you:

a. Offer just enough praise to keep them manageable.
b. Study how others handle them.
c. Flatter them to build rapport.
d. Feel awkward but try to please them.
e. Give them praise when it benefits you.

Chapter 8: Defending Against Manipulation

Emotional resilience is adapting to stress and adversity and bouncing back from setbacks with renewed strength. It embodies emotional elasticity, allowing you to recover from challenges and move forward with greater resolve. Cultivating resilience fortifies you against manipulation and enhances your capacity to manage stress and maintain mental wellbeing. Resilient individuals experience lower rates of anxiety and depression, enabling them to navigate life's ups and downs with grace and fortitude.

Developing coping mechanisms is essential for enhancing emotional resilience, providing you with tools to maintain stability even in the face of manipulation. Mindfulness and meditation are powerful practices for emotional regulation, allowing you to center yourself and remain calm amidst chaos. By focusing on the present moment without judgment, you create space for introspection and clarity, reducing the likelihood of being swayed by external influences. Cognitive-behavioral techniques further bolster resilience by helping you reframe negative thoughts and perceptions. When confronted with manipulative tactics, these techniques enable you to challenge distorted beliefs and replace them with empowering narratives. For instance, if someone attempts to undermine your confidence, cognitive restructuring allows you to recognize the manipulation for what it is and affirm your self-worth.

A cornerstone of emotional resilience is self-awareness, the ability to recognize and understand your emotions and how they influence your behavior. Self-awareness involves acknowledging the feelings that arise in response to triggers and providing insight into your vulnerabilities. Journaling exercises offer a practical means of tracking emotional patterns, enabling you to identify recurring themes and reactions. By documenting your thoughts and feelings, you gain valuable perspective on the interplay between emotions and external events. Self-reflection techniques, such as meditation or guided contemplation, enhance self-awareness by encouraging introspection. Through these practices, you cultivate a deeper understanding of your emotional landscape, equipping you to respond to manipulation with clarity and discernment.

Incorporating practical exercises into your daily routine can strengthen emotional resilience, empowering you to navigate life's challenges with confidence and poise. A daily gratitude practice is a simple yet effective way to foster a positive mindset and enhance resilience. By consciously acknowledging the aspects of your life for which you are grateful, you shift your focus from negativity to abundance, reinforcing a sense of contentment and fulfillment. Role-playing scenarios offer another valuable exercise, allowing you to practice assertiveness and boundary-setting in a safe environment. By rehearsing responses to potential manipulative situations, you build confidence in asserting your needs and protecting your wellbeing. These exercises enhance resilience and empower you to approach interactions with greater self-assurance and agency.

Self-Reflection Journaling

Set aside 10 minutes each day to reflect on your emotional experiences. Use the following questions to guide your journaling:
- What emotions did I experience today, and what triggered them?
- How did I respond to these emotions, and how did they influence my actions?
- What patterns or themes do I notice in my emotional responses?

This exercise will help you develop self-awareness, provide insights into your emotional landscape, and enhance your ability to navigate manipulation with resilience.

By cultivating emotional resilience, you'll arm yourself with the tools to withstand manipulation and emerge stronger and more empowered. You build a foundation of strength and adaptability through mindfulness, cognitive-behavioral techniques, and self-awareness practices, ensuring you can navigate life's challenges confidently and clearly. Integrating these practices into your daily life will pave the way for greater emotional wellbeing and fulfillment, empowering you to take charge of your personal development and relationships.

The Role of Emotional Intelligence in Defense

Emotional intelligence, often abbreviated as EQ, is a crucial aspect of human interaction beyond understanding one's feelings. It encompasses the ability to perceive, control, and evaluate emotions in ourselves and others. The components of EQ - self-awareness, self-regulation, social awareness, and relationship management - form the backbone of this psychological construct. Self-awareness involves recognizing one's emotions and their impact on behavior, while self-regulation is the ability to manage those emotions effectively. Social awareness requires understanding the emotional cues of others, and relationship management is about using these insights to guide interactions positively. Collectively, these skills enhance personal wellbeing and serve as powerful tools against manipulation. High emotional intelligence is often linked to personal and professional success because it allows for better problem-solving, communication, and conflict resolution. In the context of manipulation, it helps you see through deceptive facades and maintain control over your reactions, preventing others from taking advantage of emotional vulnerabilities.

Enhancing self-regulation abilities is pivotal in defending against emotional hijacking by manipulators. When faced with a situation that triggers intense emotions, it's easy to react impulsively, often to your detriment. Self-regulation equips you to pause, assess, and choose your response consciously. Techniques such as the Stop-Breathe-Reflect-Choose approach can be particularly effective. This method encourages you to take a moment to calm down, breathe deeply, and reflect on the situation before deciding how to respond. This pause allows you to shift from a reactive to a proactive stance. Calming the nervous system during heightened emotions is another key aspect of self-regulation. Techniques like deep breathing exercises or progressive muscle relaxation help soothe the body, reducing stress and anxiety. By practicing these techniques regularly, you build resilience against manipulative tactics that aim to provoke and control your emotional responses, keeping you grounded and in control.

Social awareness plays a significant role in identifying manipulative behaviors, as it involves reading social cues and understanding others' emotions. This awareness allows you to perceive subtle signals that might otherwise go unnoticed. Observing body language and micro-expressions is a critical skill in this regard. A slight change in posture or an involuntary facial expression can reveal hidden emotions and intentions, providing insights into the true nature of an interaction. For instance, a fleeting smirk or a quick glance away might indicate insincerity or discomfort. Listening skills are equally important, as they enable you to detect inconsistencies and hidden agendas in conversations. By paying close attention to tone, choice of words, and context, you can pick up on discrepancies that suggest manipulation. This heightened awareness helps you navigate interactions with greater confidence and discernment, empowering you to protect yourself from those who might seek to deceive or exploit.

Applying emotional intelligence in real-life scenarios is a practical way to strengthen your defenses against manipulation. Practicing empathy is a valuable exercise that allows you to understand others' motivations and intentions better. By putting yourself in someone else's shoes, you gain perspective on their emotional state and potential reasons for their behavior. This understanding can inform your responses, helping you engage with empathy while remaining vigilant against manipulation. Active listening exercises further enhance communication skills, fostering more meaningful and honest interactions. These exercises involve fully concentrating on the speaker, understanding their message, and responding thoughtfully. You demonstrate respect and attentiveness by engaging in active listening and building trust and rapport. This approach improves interpersonal relationships and helps you detect manipulators who rely on miscommunication and ambiguity to achieve their aims.

In conclusion, emotional intelligence is an invaluable asset in defending against manipulation. By mastering the components of EQ, you enhance your ability to recognize, understand, and manage emotions in yourself and others. This awareness empowers you to control your reactions, identify deceptive behaviors, and engage in authentic and meaningful interactions. As you continue to develop these skills, you will be better equipped to handle the complexities of human relationships and protect yourself from those who seek to manipulate you. With the knowledge you've gained, you can confidently approach the next chapter, ready to delve deeper into the strategies for recognizing manipulation in various aspects of life.

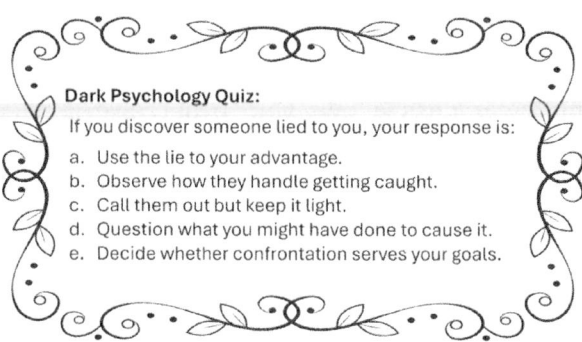

Dark Psychology Quiz:
If you discover someone lied to you, your response is:
a. Use the lie to your advantage.
b. Observe how they handle getting caught.
c. Call them out but keep it light.
d. Question what you might have done to cause it.
e. Decide whether confrontation serves your goals.

Chapter 9: Setting Boundaries Effectively

One brisk evening, as I walked along the river on the South Bank, I was deep in thought, replaying a recent encounter in my mind, where a close friend had overstepped yet again, leaving me feeling drained and disrespected. It was a familiar pattern where my reluctance to assert boundaries led to an erosion of my personal space and peace of mind. This moment by the river was pivotal, sparking a realization of the power and necessity of personal boundaries. Boundaries are invisible lines and essential constructs that safeguard your autonomy and mental health. They define where you end, and others begin, preserving your emotional and physical sanctity. Understanding personal boundaries involves recognizing their emotional, physical, and time-related forms. Emotional boundaries protect your feelings and energy, preventing others from diminishing your worth or imposing their emotions upon you. Physical boundaries delineate your comfort with personal space and physical contact, ensuring your body is respected and protected. Time-related boundaries manage your availability and how you allocate your time, preventing others from monopolizing it without regard for your needs. These boundaries are crucial in fostering healthy relationships, as they establish mutual respect and understanding, allowing connections to flourish without encroaching on your individuality.

Identifying your boundary needs is a deeply personal process shaped by your values, experiences, and comfort levels. It's about tuning into your inner voice and acknowledging what feels right for you. Start by reflecting on past interactions where you felt uncomfortable or violated. Consider what about those situations felt wrong and what could have been done differently. Reflective exercises can be invaluable in this process, helping you assess your personal limits and boundaries. Take time to journal about these experiences, exploring the emotions and thoughts they evoke. You might ask yourself: "When have I felt overwhelmed by others' demands?" or "What are the recurring patterns of discomfort in my relationships?" These prompts can uncover insights into where your boundaries lie and how they have been challenged. By understanding these patterns, you can articulate your boundary needs with clarity and confidence.

Communicating your boundaries is essential for ensuring that others respect and understand them. This requires a combination of assertiveness and empathy, allowing you to express your needs without alienating those around you. One effective strategy is to use "I" statements, which focus on your feelings and needs rather than blaming or accusing others. For example, saying, "I need some time to myself in the evenings to recharge," is more constructive than, "You always take up all my time." Practicing assertive communication techniques can also bolster your ability to convey boundaries effectively. Assertiveness involves expressing your needs openly and honestly while maintaining respect for others. It requires a balance of confidence and consideration, ensuring your message is received without hostility or defensiveness. Developing scripts for common boundary-setting scenarios can also be helpful. Think about situations where you frequently need to assert boundaries, such as declining additional responsibilities at work or setting limits on social engagements. Prepare responses that convey your needs clearly, such as "I appreciate the offer, but I need to focus on my current commitments." These preparations can reduce anxiety and empower you to uphold your boundaries consistently.

Handling boundary violations is a crucial aspect of maintaining your autonomy and self-respect. Violations can range from minor breaches, like a friend showing up unannounced, to more severe intrusions, such as persistent unwanted contact. Addressing these violations requires a thoughtful approach that balances firmness with understanding. For minor breaches, a gentle reminder of your boundaries may suffice. You might say, "I enjoy our time together, but I prefer if we plan visits ahead of time." This reinforces your boundary while maintaining the relationship's integrity. For repeated or severe violations, a more assertive response may be necessary. Clearly state the crossed boundary and its impact on you, such as "When you call late at night, it disrupts my sleep. I need you to respect my request for no calls after 9pm." It's essential to remain calm and composed, avoiding overly emotional reactions that might escalate the situation. Reinforcing boundaries without guilt is another key strategy. It's natural to feel uncomfortable asserting yourself, especially if you fear conflict or rejection. However, remember that setting boundaries is an act of self-care and respect. It's about honoring your needs and ensuring equitable and fulfilling relationships. Practice self-compassion and remind yourself that it's okay to prioritize your wellbeing.

Boundary Identification Exercise

Take a moment to sit quietly and reflect on a recent interaction where your boundaries were challenged. In a journal, jot down the details of the situation, your emotional response, and what boundary was crossed. Next, write a response you wish you had given, using "I" statements to express your needs. Consider how this exercise can guide future boundary-setting efforts.

By embracing the power of personal boundaries, you create a foundation for healthier, more respectful relationships. Through reflection, communication, and assertiveness, you can uphold your autonomy and foster connections that honor your individuality. As you continue to explore the dynamics of boundaries, remember that this journey is a testament to your commitment to self-respect and emotional wellbeing.

Maintaining Professional Boundaries

In the bustling environment of today's workplaces, maintaining professional boundaries can often feel like walking a tightrope. These boundaries are not just about protecting personal space but are vital for ensuring respect, productivity, and a healthy work-life balance. They serve as invisible lines that define what is acceptable in professional interactions, helping to prevent burnout and stress. When these lines blur, the consequences can be overwhelming. Imagine constantly being bombarded with work emails at midnight or feeling pressured to attend meetings during your personal time; such scenarios can quickly deplete your energy and affect your mental wellbeing. Professional boundaries safeguard against this erosion, allowing you to recharge and perform at your best. In different workplace settings, these boundaries manifest in various forms. For instance, respecting personal space and minimizing distractions are crucial in an open-plan office. Conversely, delineating work hours from personal time becomes paramount in remote work environments. Establishing clear boundaries creates an atmosphere where everyone knows what to expect, fostering mutual respect and collaboration.

Establishing boundaries with colleagues and supervisors is an essential skill that can transform your work environment into one that is both respectful and collaborative. It begins with setting limits on after-hours communication. While it might be tempting to respond to emails or messages immediately, it's important to define clear time boundaries. Communicate your availability and stick to it. For example, let your team know you won't check work emails after a certain hour unless it's an emergency. This not only respects your personal time but also sets a precedent for others to follow. Another aspect is defining personal space in shared work environments. Whether it's an open office or a shared desk, having a designated area you can call your own helps maintain focus and efficiency. Politely request colleagues to respect this space, perhaps by using visual cues like putting your earphones in, indicating when you're in deep work mode. Handling requests that exceed your job responsibilities is also crucial. It's not uncommon for roles to expand beyond their original scope, but that doesn't mean you should always say yes. Evaluate each request based on your current workload and career goals, and don't hesitate to decline tasks that stretch your limits. Maintaining these boundaries fosters a culture of respect and understanding that enhances collaboration.

Navigating boundary challenges in the workplace is something everyone encounters at some point. From boundary pushers who persistently test your limits to managing requests that seem never-ending, these challenges require a strategic approach. Addressing boundary pushers involves a firm yet diplomatic stance. When faced with a colleague who consistently oversteps, it's important to reiterate your boundaries with clarity and assertiveness. For instance, if someone frequently interrupts you during focused work time, a simple, "I'm in the middle of a task right now; could we discuss this later?" can be effective. Balancing assertiveness with teamwork and flexibility is another key aspect. While standing your ground is important, being a team player often involves compromise. The focus should be on finding a balance where your boundaries are respected, yet you remain open to collaboration. Flexibility doesn't mean compromising your values but adjusting where necessary without losing sight of your priorities.

To reinforce professional boundaries consistently, you can leverage various tools and practices that support your efforts. Time management techniques are invaluable for upholding work-life balance. Consider adopting methods like time blocking, where you allocate specific times for tasks and breaks, ensuring a structured workday. This not only boosts productivity but also reinforces your commitment to personal time. Leveraging workplace policies can also be a powerful ally. Familiarise yourself with your organisation's policies on work hours, overtime, and communication. These policies can provide a framework that supports your boundary-setting efforts, giving you an official basis to refer to when needed. Seeking mentorship or support from HR is another effective strategy when boundaries are challenged. Mentors can offer guidance and share experiences in navigating similar situations, while HR can provide resources and support to address any persistent boundary issues. Utilising these tools creates an environment where boundaries are respected, allowing you to thrive personally and professionally.

It's also helpful to establish language that communicates your boundaries clearly and confidently. Simple phrases like "I'll respond during work hours," or "I'm not available for meetings after 5pm," can become part of your regular vocabulary, reinforcing expectations without apology. Practising assertive communication, especially when requests cross a line, helps prevent future oversteps. The more consistent you are, the more others learn to respect your limits - not because they're forced to, but because you've modelled clarity, fairness, and professionalism.

Finally, remember that maintaining boundaries is a continuous practice, not a one-time declaration. As roles evolve, teams shift, and responsibilities grow, your boundaries may need to adapt too. Periodically reassess what's working and what feels stretched, and don't be afraid to adjust. By treating boundaries as a living part of your professional identity, you create a sustainable rhythm that protects your energy, sharpens your focus, and honours your worth.

As we draw this chapter to a close, it's evident that maintaining professional boundaries is not just about drawing lines but building a work environment that respects and nurtures your wellbeing. Boundaries are integral to sustaining a healthy balance between work and life, ensuring professional and personal growth. As we transition to the next chapter, we'll delve deeper into understanding psychological warfare and how these strategies can further enhance your ability to navigate complex dynamics with resilience and confidence.

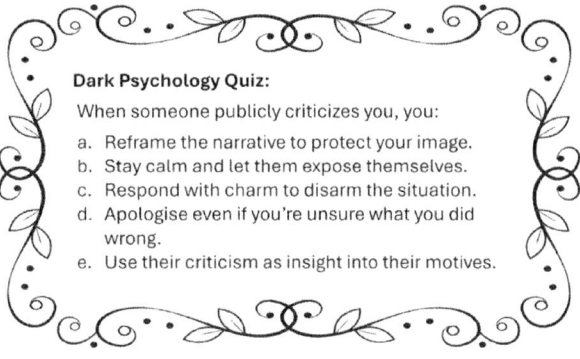

Dark Psychology Quiz:

When someone publicly criticizes you, you:

a. Reframe the narrative to protect your image.
b. Stay calm and let them expose themselves.
c. Respond with charm to disarm the situation.
d. Apologise even if you're unsure what you did wrong.
e. Use their criticism as insight into their motives.

Chapter 10: Healing and Moving Forward

Each wave In the aftermath of manipulative relationships, the path to healing is not linear but a unique journey of rediscovery and resilience. Understanding the lingering impact of manipulation is essential. It often leaves traces of chronic self-doubt and a fragmented sense of identity. You may question your decisions, wondering if you can trust your intuition. Anxiety becomes a frequent companion, manifesting as hyper-vigilance in new interactions. It's as if your mind, once a sanctuary, has become a labyrinth of caution and skepticism.

Acknowledging and processing these complex emotions is a significant step toward emotional healing. Creating a safe space to explore these feelings without judgment is vital. Journaling offers a private sanctuary for emotional exploration. By putting pen to paper, you can untangle the web of emotions that manipulation has woven. This practice allows you to gain insight into your experiences, releasing pent-up emotions and gaining clarity. Guided meditations focusing on emotional release can further support this process. You can gently confront and release the emotions that hold you captive through mindfulness, making space for healing and renewal. I've personally found the Calm app to be very helpful for this. Artistic expression is a therapeutic outlet through painting, music, or dance. It allows you to express what words cannot capture, transforming pain into beauty and fostering a sense of empowerment.

Developing healthy coping mechanisms is crucial in replacing maladaptive habits that may have formed during manipulative relationships. Mindfulness practices, such as meditation or deep breathing exercises, help reduce stress and anxiety by anchoring you in the present moment. These practices cultivate a sense of calm and control, counteracting the chaos that manipulation often leaves behind. Engaging in physical activities like yoga or dance can also be profoundly healing. These activities enable you to reconnect with your body, releasing tension and fostering a sense of vitality. The rhythm and flow of movement provide an opportunity to express and process emotions, promoting a sense of liberation and peace.

Seeking professional help is an important step in your healing journey, particularly when the burden of past experiences feels overwhelming. Therapy offers a structured environment where you can explore your emotions, identify patterns, and develop strategies for healing. Finding a therapist who specializes in trauma recovery is paramount. They possess the expertise to guide you through the complexities of your experiences, offering support and insight tailored to your needs. Support groups provide a community of individuals who share similar experiences, creating a space for shared healing and understanding. These groups offer validation and solidarity, reminding you that you are not alone in your struggle.

In recent years, online therapy has become a convenient and accessible option for many. Platforms like BetterHelp and Talkspace provide flexible scheduling and a variety of therapeutic modalities, making it easier to find a therapist who aligns with your preferences. Online therapy can be particularly beneficial if you face barriers to in-person sessions, such as geographical constraints or time limitations. This format offers a sense of privacy and comfort, allowing you to engage in therapy safely in your own space.

Journaling for Emotional Exploration

Consider the following prompt for your next journaling session: "Reflect on a moment when you felt manipulated or controlled. How did it affect your emotions and self-perception? What did you learn about yourself from this experience, and how can you use this insight to foster healing and growth?" Allow yourself to write freely, without judgment, and explore the arising emotions. This exercise can help you process your experiences and uncover insights guiding your healing path.

As you embark on this healing journey, remember that every step you take is a testament to your strength and resilience. Embrace the process with patience and self-compassion, knowing that healing is not a destination but a continuous journey of growth and transformation. The scars of manipulation may linger, but they do not define you. Instead, they remind you of your courage and the unwavering light within you, ready to shine brighter than ever before.

Rebuilding Trust and Confidence

Rebuilding trust in oneself and others can feel daunting after experiencing manipulation. Yet, it's a crucial step toward reclaiming control over your life. Trust cannot be restored overnight; it requires patience and self-compassion. Begin by setting small, achievable goals that allow trust to develop gradually. For instance, start by trusting yourself to make minor decisions without second-guessing. This might involve simple choices like selecting a meal or planning a day out. As you become more comfortable, extend this trust to more significant decisions. Engaging in trust-building activities with close friends or family can also be beneficial. These activities, such as group projects or shared hobbies, create opportunities to rebuild trust in a safe and supportive environment. Through these interactions, you can learn to rely on others again, knowing that the bonds you form are grounded in mutual respect and care.

Strengthening self-confidence is equally important in this journey. Confidence is the foundation upon which trust is built, and nurturing it requires deliberate effort. Start by incorporating daily affirmations into your routine to reinforce positive self-beliefs. These affirmations, statements like "I am capable" or "I am worthy of love," can gradually shift your mindset from doubt to self-assurance. Celebrate small victories and milestones, no matter how insignificant they may seem. Did you complete a challenging task at work or stick to a new habit for a week? Recognize these achievements and allow them to bolster your confidence. Visualization exercises can also play a decisive role in strengthening self-confidence. Picture yourself succeeding in future endeavors, whether acing a presentation or navigating a social event easily. By imagining these scenarios, you train your mind to anticipate success, making it more likely to become a reality.

Creating a supportive environment is vital for nurturing trust and confidence. Surround yourself with positive, supportive individuals encouraging growth and understanding of your journey. These relationships are a buffer against self-doubt and reinforce your belief in your capabilities. Equally important is organizing your personal space to reflect calm and security. A tidy, inviting environment can significantly impact your mental state, providing a sanctuary where you feel safe and at ease. Consider incorporating elements that bring you joy, such as plants, artwork, or soothing colors. These small touches can transform your space into a haven that nurtures your sense of wellbeing. Keeping your living spaces tidy and clean also helps keep your mind at bay.

Embracing new experiences is another powerful way to build confidence and trust in yourself. Stepping outside your comfort zone can be intimidating, but it's also an opportunity for growth. Trying new hobbies or activities can introduce you to new skills and perspectives. Whether taking a dance class, learning a new language, or exploring a creative pursuit, these experiences can boost your self-esteem and expand your horizons. Volunteering or community involvement is another avenue for growth. Engaging with others in a meaningful way not only broadens your perspective but also reinforces your sense of purpose and connection. Additionally, traveling or exploring new cultures can challenge existing beliefs and encourage adaptability. These experiences can teach resilience and confidence as you navigate unfamiliar environments and interactions with curiosity and openness.

In rebuilding trust and confidence, remember that each step you take is a testament to your resilience and strength. Embrace the process with patience and kindness toward yourself, knowing that growth is a gradual and rewarding endeavor. As you continue to build these foundations, you'll find that the world opens up with new possibilities and connections, ready to be explored with renewed trust in yourself and those around you. With these tools at your disposal, you're well-equipped to navigate the complexities of life, cultivating relationships and experiences that enrich your journey.

As you move forward, consider how these insights can be applied to broader aspects of your life. The next chapter will delve deeper into real-life applications of these principles, offering practical guidance for navigating relationships and environments with confidence and integrity.

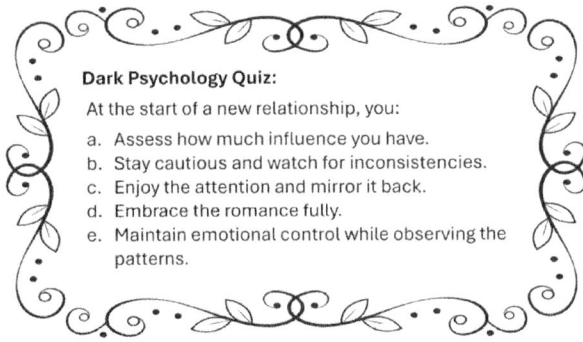

Dark Psychology Quiz:
At the start of a new relationship, you:
a. Assess how much influence you have.
b. Stay cautious and watch for inconsistencies.
c. Enjoy the attention and mirror it back.
d. Embrace the romance fully.
e. Maintain emotional control while observing the patterns.

Chapter 11: Real-Life Scenarios

Throughout history, manipulation has played pivotal roles in various contexts, leaving indelible marks on society. Consider the world of espionage, where psychological warfare tactics have been wielded with precision. According to the CIA's 'The Psychology of Espionage,' spies often use deception and manipulation to extract information or influence outcomes. In high-profile espionage cases, agents employ psychological tactics to gain trust, exploit vulnerabilities, and manipulate emotions. These tactics, while effective, often lead to long-term consequences for both the manipulators and their targets. The psychological toll on individuals involved can be immense, leaving scars that linger long after the dust has settled.

Project MKUltra was a covert CIA program that ran from 1953 to 1973, designed to develop mind control techniques through a combination of drugs, psychological manipulation, and extreme interrogation methods. Conducted without the consent of many of its subjects, the program employed tactics such as high doses of LSD, hypnosis, sensory deprivation, electroshock therapy, and other forms of psychological and physical abuse, all aimed at breaking down and controlling the human mind. Widely condemned as a severe abuse of power, it is one of the most infamous examples of government-sponsored experimentation.

The program was managed through the CIA's Office of Scientific Intelligence, often disguised under front organizations to conceal its true purpose. More than 80 institutions, including universities, hospitals, and prisons, were involved, and experiments were conducted on informed and unwitting subjects across the United States and Canada.

The existence of MKUltra came to light in 1975, thanks to investigations by the Church Committee and the Rockefeller Commission. However, efforts to uncover the full scope of the program were obstructed when most official records were deliberately destroyed in 1973. A breakthrough came in 1977, when a Freedom of Information Act request unearthed 20,000 previously undisclosed documents, prompting Senate hearings into the program. Additional files were partially declassified in 2001, but much of MKUltra's dark legacy remains shrouded in secrecy.

In the corporate realm, manipulation is standard, as evidenced by numerous accounting scandals. Executives have been known to manipulate financial statements to mislead investors and shareholders, ultimately leading to disastrous outcomes. In 2001, the energy giant Enron collapsed into bankruptcy after it was exposed for concealing billions in debt through fraudulent accounting practices. The fallout didn't just destroy Enron - it also triggered the dismantling of Arthur Andersen, one of the world's largest and most respected accounting firms, after its complicity in covering up Enron's financial misconduct came to light.

Such scandals highlight how individuals will deceive and exploit for financial gain. The manipulation of financial data creates a false sense of security, only to unravel when the truth comes to light. These cases are stark reminders of the importance of transparency and accountability in business practices. The ripple effects of these scandals extend beyond financial losses, eroding trust and confidence in corporate leadership.

Interpersonal manipulation takes on different forms, often manifesting in complex relationship dynamics. This tactic, characterized by denial and contradiction, erodes self-trust and leaves individuals vulnerable to further manipulation. Love bombing, usually seen in high-stakes business negotiations, involves overwhelming an individual with attention and praise to gain loyalty and compliance. Initially, this tactic creates a sense of euphoria, but it often leads to disappointment and disillusionment when promises aren't fulfilled. Emotional blackmail within familial dynamics can be equally damaging, as family members use guilt and obligation to manipulate behavior, creating a cycle of dependency and control.

Till death do us part - or so the saying goes. However, for Queen Victoria, death was far from the end regarding her connection with Prince Albert. After Albert died in 1861, just months after Victoria's mother also passed, the queen sank into a deep and unrelenting mourning. In keeping with Victorian tradition, she wore mourning jewelry, small tokens holding tiny photographs of Albert, and even locks of his hair, keeping physical reminders of him close at all times. What she didn't realize, however, was that these pieces might hold more power than simple sentiment.

At the height of her grief, a young psychic medium - only 13 years old - was introduced to the queen. The boy claimed to be able to speak with Albert's spirit, and during a séance, Victoria heard something that left her stunned. Speaking through the boy, Albert's voice used a pet name only the two of them had ever known. There was no doubt in her mind - it was him.

From that moment on, the grieving queen found comfort in her mourning rituals and these supernatural connections. The boy became a regular guest at Buckingham Palace and was summoned to hold séances where Victoria could continue to consult Albert's spirit. According to some accounts, she even sought his advice on political matters, blurring the line between earthly governance and the whisperings of the dead.

The lessons learned from these cases are invaluable. They underscore the importance of support networks in overcoming manipulation. Surrounding yourself with trusted friends, family, or colleagues can provide the validation and perspective needed to break free from manipulative dynamics. These networks offer a lifeline, reminding you of your worth and reinforcing your ability to make sound decisions. Techniques for regaining trust and credibility after manipulation also emerge from these cases. Rebuilding trust requires patience, transparency, and a commitment to consistent, honest communication. Demonstrating accountability and taking responsibility for one's actions fosters an environment where trust can be rebuilt over time.

Applying insights from these case studies to your own life can foster a deeper understanding and preparedness for dealing with manipulation. Reflective questions can help assess personal experiences, such as, "Have I encountered similar manipulation tactics in my relationships or workplace?" and "How can I strengthen my support network to resist manipulation?" Journaling about these reflections can provide clarity and guide you in developing strategies to address manipulation. Exercises that develop critical thinking and awareness from case study learnings can be invaluable.

Journaling for Self-Reflection

Reflect on a situation where you felt manipulated or pressured into a decision. Write about the tactics used and how they made you feel. Consider the support system you had at the time and how it affected your response. What lessons can you draw from this experience to strengthen your ability to recognize and resist manipulation in the future? Use this prompt as a tool to build awareness and resilience against manipulation.

Understanding real-life manipulation scenarios equips you with the knowledge and skills to navigate complex interactions confidently. By learning from historical cases and interpersonal examples, you can anticipate and counteract manipulation in your life, fostering healthier relationships and environments.

Practical Applications for Everyday Life

Think about a casual gathering with friends or acquaintances, where the atmosphere is light and laughter flows freely. Yet beneath this surface, manipulation can quietly weave its way into interactions. In social settings, peer pressure is a familiar form of manipulation many encounter. Whether it's the subtle coercion to conform to group norms or the more overt pressure to partake in activities you might not be comfortable with, handling peer pressure requires both awareness and assertiveness. It's important to recognize when you're being nudged into decisions that don't align with your values. One effective strategy is to practice saying "no" confidently without extensively explaining your decision. You can maintain your integrity while navigating social dynamics by setting clear personal boundaries.

When I had my first baby, I expected the sleepless nights and the endless nappy changes. What wasn't apparent was the unspoken pressure from other mums to parent a certain way. At our local baby group, conversations quickly turned into subtle comparisons - whose baby was sleeping through the night, who was breastfeeding exclusively, and who had already started baby sign language classes.

At first, I brushed it off, telling myself every baby is different. But the more I heard, the more I felt the weight of other mothers' choices pressing down on my own. Was I failing because I hadn't made my own pureed food? Was my baby behind developmentally because we hadn't signed up for sensory classes? The fear of judgment and exclusion made me second-guess my instincts, even when they worked perfectly well for the baby and me.

Peer pressure doesn't disappear after school - it evolves, showing up in mum groups, online forums, and playground chats. It can leave new mums feeling inadequate, isolated, and anxious, all because they're trying to fit into someone else's definition of the 'perfect mother' rather than trusting their own instincts. Recognizing this pressure is the first step toward letting it go - because the truth is, there's no one right way to raise a baby, no matter what the crowd says.

Another common challenge in social gatherings is dealing with passive-aggressive behavior. This might manifest as backhanded compliments or veiled criticisms that unsettle you. Addressing such behavior directly yet tactfully can diffuse tension and clarify intentions. Acknowledging the comment and asking for clarification often exposes the underlying issue, allowing for open dialogue rather than festering resentment.

In consumer interactions, manipulation often takes on a more strategic form. Sales and marketing tactics are designed to persuade you to make purchases, sometimes using pressure tactics to create a sense of urgency. Think of the salesperson who insists that a deal is only available for a limited time, pushing you to act hastily. Recognizing these tactics allows you to take a step back and evaluate your needs independently. It's helpful to ask for time to consider your options, ensuring that decisions are made from a place of clarity rather than pressure. Similarly, customer service can sometimes turn manipulative, using charm to placate dissatisfaction without addressing the root issue. When encountering this, focus on expressing your concerns clearly and assertively, requesting specific solutions rather than accepting vague promises. By maintaining a firm stance, you can ensure your needs are met without succumbing to manipulative tactics.

Enhancing personal relationships involves recognizing and addressing manipulative behaviors that may undermine trust and connection. Clear communication channels are essential to prevent misunderstandings that can lead to conflict. Establishing a routine of open dialogue, where both parties feel heard and respected, fosters a deeper bond and reduces the likelihood of manipulation taking root. Practicing empathy and active listening further strengthens these bonds. By truly understanding the perspectives and emotions of those you care about, you create a supportive environment where manipulation has little room to thrive. This practice not only reinforces trust but also encourages mutual respect and understanding. Building relationships on a foundation of empathy and communication empowers you to navigate challenges collaboratively, enhancing the overall quality of your interactions.

Creating a personal action plan to address manipulation in your daily life is a proactive approach that empowers you with tailored solutions. Begin by setting specific goals for boundary-setting and communication. Identify areas where you feel most vulnerable to manipulation and outline clear strategies to protect your interests. Regularly reviewing and adjusting these strategies based on personal experiences ensures they remain effective and relevant. Engaging in self-reflection is a crucial aspect of this process. Examining past interactions and identifying patterns can refine your approach to future situations. Seeking feedback from trusted sources also provides valuable insights. This ongoing process of reflection and adjustment is key to maintaining autonomy and resilience in the face of manipulation.

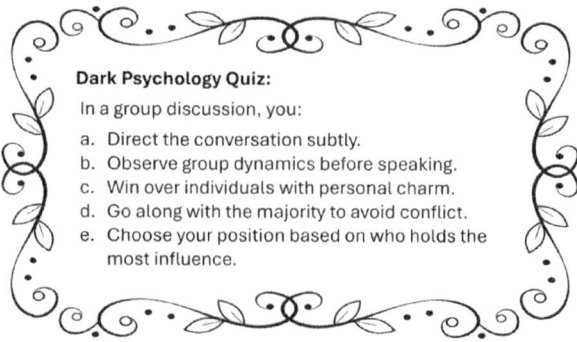

Dark Psychology Quiz:

In a group discussion, you:
a. Direct the conversation subtly.
b. Observe group dynamics before speaking.
c. Win over individuals with personal charm.
d. Go along with the majority to avoid conflict.
e. Choose your position based on who holds the most influence.

Chapter 12: Empowerment through Knowledge

The concept of social proof, introduced by Robert Cialdini, explains how individuals often look to others to determine their actions, especially in uncertain situations. This phenomenon is a cornerstone of influence, suggesting that when people see others engaging in a behavior, they are likelier to do the same. For example, online reviews and testimonials are powerful forms of social proof that shape consumer behavior. When you see a product with thousands of positive reviews, you feel more confident in its quality, even if you are initially unsure. Social proof can manifest subtly in everyday life, such as when you choose a busy restaurant over an empty one, assuming the crowd signifies quality. This reliance on others' behavior as a guide to appropriate action underscores the impact of social proof on decision-making.

Reciprocity, another foundational theory, plays a critical role in persuasion by leveraging the human tendency to repay kindness and favors. This principle suggests you feel obligated to return the favor when someone does something for you. Marketers often use this tactic by offering free samples or gifts, knowing that the gesture increases the likelihood of a purchase. In personal relationships, reciprocity builds trust and strengthens bonds, as acts of kindness and support create a cycle of giving and receiving. This powerful motivator can be both a tool for goodwill and a mechanism for influence, as individuals are more likely to comply with requests from those who have previously helped them. Recognizing the impact of reciprocity allows you to navigate social interactions with greater awareness, understanding how gestures of goodwill can shape behavior and responses.

The concept of authority significantly influences compliance, highlighting the power of perceived expertise or status in guiding behavior. This principle suggests that people are more likely to follow the lead of someone they perceive as knowledgeable or in a position of authority. In a professional setting, a manager's directive may carry more weight simply because of their title. This dynamic can be seen in advertising when experts, such as doctors or scientists, endorse products, lending credibility and encouraging trust. The authority effect is powerful because it taps into the human tendency to defer to those who appear to know more, often bypassing critical evaluation. Understanding this principle equips you to question authority figures and assess whether their influence aligns with your values and judgment.

Cognitive dissonance, a theory explored in political and consumer behavior, reveals how individuals strive for internal consistency between beliefs and actions to avoid psychological discomfort. This phenomenon occurs when there's a conflict between beliefs or between beliefs and behavior, prompting individuals to adjust their attitudes or actions to resolve the tension. In advertising, this theory is often used to encourage brand loyalty. For instance, if you've invested in a product, you're more likely to seek information reinforcing your purchase decision, minimizing regret or doubt. Political campaigns also exploit cognitive dissonance by aligning messages with voters' existing beliefs, encouraging them to support candidates whose platforms resonate with their values, even when faced with contrary evidence. Recognizing cognitive dissonance in action allows you to critically assess your beliefs and decisions, ensuring they are based on genuine understanding rather than needing consistency.

The foot-in-the-door technique exemplifies how small commitments can lead to more extensive compliance through gradual escalation. This strategy involves securing a minor agreement as a precursor to a more significant request. For example, during door-to-door sales, a salesperson might first ask you to answer a few questions, creating a sense of engagement. You will likely consider purchasing the product once you agree to this small request. Charitable organizations often use this approach by initially seeking a small donation or commitment, which, once made, increases the likelihood of continued or more significant contributions. This technique underscores the power of incremental commitment in shaping behavior and decisions, highlighting the importance of being mindful of initial agreements and their potential implications.

In daily life, understanding these psychological theories of influence empowers you to recognize and counteract undue pressure. For instance, developing resistance to persuasive sales tactics involves questioning initial offers and considering long-term implications before committing. Awareness of subtle persuasion in social interactions helps you maintain autonomy in decision-making, ensuring your choices reflect your values and priorities. By applying these insights, you can confidently navigate influence, making informed decisions that align with your true intentions and desires. This awareness protects you from manipulation and fosters a deeper understanding of the dynamics that shape human behavior.

The Empowerment of Self-Knowledge

The path to understanding oneself is paved with moments of introspection and reflection. As you navigate this terrain, you uncover layers of your identity, each revelation offering a clearer picture of who you are and what you value. Self-discovery is more than a fleeting exercise; it is a profound process that empowers you to live authentically. Reflective practices, such as journaling or meditation, are valuable tools in this endeavor. You cultivate a deeper awareness of your inner world by setting aside time to contemplate your experiences and emotions. This practice enhances self-awareness and fortifies your ability to navigate life's challenges with clarity and intention.

Identifying your personal values and beliefs forms the cornerstone of self-awareness. These core principles guide your actions and decisions, offering a moral compass that anchors you in times of uncertainty. Through introspection, you gain insight into what truly matters to you: integrity, compassion, or ambition. This understanding empowers you to make choices that align with your values, fostering a sense of congruence between your beliefs and actions. Recognizing your strengths and weaknesses further enriches this journey. By acknowledging your talents and areas for growth, you position yourself to leverage your strengths while addressing your challenges. This balanced perspective promotes self-acceptance, encouraging you to embrace and use your unique qualities to your advantage.

Tools for self-assessment offer structured approaches to understanding your personality and preferences. Assessments like the Myers-Briggs Type Indicator provide insights into your cognitive functions and how you interact with the world. By revealing your personality type, these tools illuminate your natural inclinations, helping you understand how you engage with others and process information. Emotional intelligence evaluations are equally enlightening, measuring your ability to perceive, understand, and manage emotions. This awareness is crucial for developing empathy and effective communication skills, both essential components of healthy relationships. These assessments are not merely diagnostic but empowering tools that equip you with the knowledge to navigate social dynamics confidently and authentically.

The impact of self-knowledge on decision-making is profound, as it informs choices that are not only informed but also deeply aligned with your true self. When you understand your values and strengths, you can set personal goals that reflect your aspirations and priorities. This alignment ensures that your pursuits are meaningful and fulfilling, enhancing your motivation and determination. Regarding career decisions, self-knowledge plays a pivotal role in guiding your path. By choosing roles and environments that resonate with your values, you create a work life that is satisfying and purpose-driven. This intentional decision-making fosters a sense of fulfillment and reduces the likelihood of burnout, as your professional endeavors are grounded in authenticity.

Self-knowledge is not a static achievement but a dynamic, lifelong process of growth and evolution. Cultivating continuous self-improvement requires a commitment to ongoing learning and reflection. Keeping a personal growth journal is a powerful tool in this pursuit, as it provides a space to document your thoughts, goals, and progress. This practice encourages regular self-reflection, allowing you to track your development and celebrate your achievements. Setting aside dedicated time for introspection through meditation or quiet contemplation reinforces this growth-oriented mindset. Additionally, seeking feedback from trusted mentors and peers offers valuable perspectives that can illuminate blind spots and enhance your understanding of yourself. This external input, coupled with your self-reflective efforts, creates a comprehensive picture of your strengths and opportunities for growth.

As you embrace the empowerment of self-knowledge, consider how these insights can transform your interactions and decisions. You can face challenges confidently and clearly with a deeper understanding of your values and strengths. This chapter invites you to explore the depths of your identity, recognizing that each insight gained is a step toward living an authentic life.

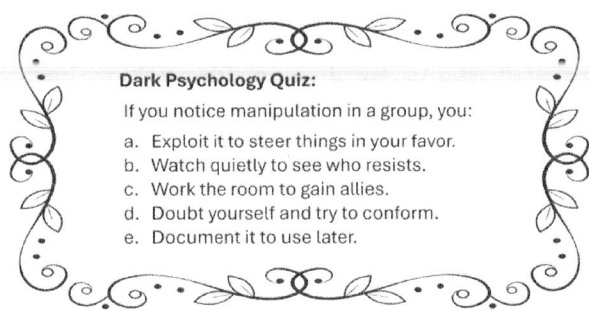

Dark Psychology Quiz:
If you notice manipulation in a group, you:
a. Exploit it to steer things in your favor.
b. Watch quietly to see who resists.
c. Work the room to gain allies.
d. Doubt yourself and try to conform.
e. Document it to use later.

Chapter 13: Exploring Emotional Intelligence

Navigating joy, anger, sadness, and everything in between requires more than cognitive ability; it demands emotional intelligence (EQ). This form of intelligence is not about what you know in terms of facts and figures. It's about understanding the subtle currents of emotions influencing your daily actions and interactions. Emotional intelligence is your ability to perceive, understand, and manage emotions effectively. It allows you to connect with others, resolve conflicts, and lead a fulfilling life.

Emotional intelligence plays a significant role in both personal and professional contexts. It strongly predicts success and wellbeing, often surpassing traditional cognitive intelligence (IQ) in its impact on life outcomes. While IQ measures your ability to solve problems and understand complex ideas, EQ focuses on your ability to navigate social complexities and make personal decisions that achieve positive results. Research indicates that EQ is crucial for fostering understanding, empathy, and effective communication in relationships, making it essential for anyone looking to thrive in today's interconnected world.

According to Daniel Goleman, the emotional intelligence framework is built on five key components. First, self-awareness is the bedrock of emotional intelligence. It involves recognizing your emotions as they occur, understanding their effect on your thoughts and behavior, and acknowledging how they influence your interactions. Knowing your feelings, you can better control your reactions and avoid being overwhelmed by them. This self-awareness leads seamlessly into self-regulation, which is the ability to manage your emotional responses. Secondly, self-regulation allows you to pause before reacting, ensuring your actions align with your values and long-term goals. It helps you maintain control, even when faced with stressful situations or provocation.

Motivation is another pillar of emotional intelligence. The drive compels you to pursue your goals with enthusiasm and persistence. Unlike external rewards, intrinsic motivation is fueled by your inner desires and passions. This component of EQ helps you stay focused, resilient, and optimistic, even in the face of setbacks. When you're motivated, you're more likely to take initiative and remain committed to your objectives. Next, empathy is the capacity to understand and share the feelings of others. It allows you to connect with people more profoundly, fostering trust and rapport. By putting yourself in someone else's shoes, you gain insight into their perspective, which enhances your ability to communicate effectively and resolve conflicts. Finally, social skills are the tools that enable you to build and maintain healthy relationships. Whether through active listening, clear communication, or conflict resolution, strong social skills help you easily navigate complex social landscapes.

The benefits of high emotional intelligence extend far beyond personal satisfaction. In professional settings, individuals with strong EQ tend to excel in leadership roles, as they can communicate clearly, inspire and motivate teams, and manage conflicts with tact and diplomacy. Their enhanced communication skills allow them to articulate their ideas persuasively and build consensus among diverse groups. Furthermore, high emotional intelligence contributes to resilience in the face of stress and emotional challenges. Those who possess it are better equipped to cope with adversity, adapt to change, and maintain composure under pressure. This resilience improves workplace performance and enhances overall wellbeing and life satisfaction.

While emotional and cognitive intelligence play vital roles in human functioning, they serve distinct purposes. Cognitive intelligence, or IQ, is often associated with logical reasoning, problem-solving, and analytical skills. It provides the framework for understanding complex concepts and making informed decisions. However, EQ complements IQ by guiding interpersonal interactions and shaping how you engage with the world emotionally and socially. While IQ might help you design a brilliant strategy, EQ ensures you can communicate it effectively and garner the support needed to bring it to fruition. These two forms of intelligence are intertwined, each enhancing the other's effectiveness and contributing to a more balanced and rewarding life.

Assessing Your Emotional Intelligence

Take a moment to reflect on your emotional intelligence. Consider situations where you successfully managed your emotions or empathized with others. What strengths do you notice? Are there areas where you'd like to improve? Jot down your thoughts in a journal and consider how to apply these insights to enhance your personal and professional life. This exercise can provide clarity on your emotional strengths and areas for growth.

Understanding emotional intelligence (EQ) is not just a theoretical exercise - it's a practical tool that can transform your interactions and relationships. By honing your EQ, you can enhance your communication skills, strengthen your leadership abilities, and improve your overall quality of life. As we explore emotional intelligence further, consider how these insights can be integrated into your daily life, fostering a more empathetic and connected existence.

Developing Emotional Awareness

Recognizing emotions as they arise allows you to understand their origins and predict their impact on your behavior and interactions. When you can name what you're feeling - anger, joy, frustration - you begin to demystify your emotional world. This clarity acts as a guide, helping you navigate complex social landscapes with greater ease and confidence.

Emotional triggers, those stimuli that provoke a strong emotional response, are crucial in shaping how you react to the world. Understanding these triggers can seem daunting, but managing your responses effectively is essential. An offhand comment from a colleague stings, not because of the words themselves, but because they echo past criticisms you've received. By identifying such triggers, you gain control over your reactions, transforming potential conflict into opportunities for growth and understanding. This awareness empowers you to respond rather than react, offering a moment of reflection between stimulus and response.

Cultivating emotional awareness requires deliberate practice and patience. Mindfulness meditation is one effective technique that allows you to observe your emotions without judgment. Picture yourself sitting quietly, focusing on your breath, and simply acknowledging emotions as they surface - like clouds passing through the sky. This practice nurtures a non-reactive mindset, where you learn to witness emotions without being swept away. Regular meditation can increase your emotional insight, providing a calm space to explore your feelings and their origins.

Journaling is a valuable tool for enhancing emotional awareness. By writing about your daily emotional experiences, you create a record that helps you track patterns and identify recurring themes. Consider each entry a snapshot of your emotional landscape, capturing the highs and lows with honesty and reflection. Over time, these snapshots form a narrative that reveals how your emotions influence your decisions and relationships. This process clarifies your emotional state and offers a therapeutic outlet for processing complex feelings.

Deep breathing exercises are another strategy for calming the mind and enhancing emotional insight. When emotions threaten to overwhelm you, a few deep breaths can ground you, creating a momentary pause that disrupts the cycle of automatic reactions. Focus on the rhythm of your breath, allowing each inhale and exhale to anchor you in the present.

This practice not only soothes the mind but also provides the clarity needed to assess your emotions objectively.

Recognizing emotional patterns is key to understanding how past experiences shape your present responses. Reflect on relationships and interactions, noting any recurring emotional themes. Do certain dynamics consistently evoke feelings of insecurity or resentment? Understanding these patterns helps you identify areas for growth and healing. Past trauma, in particular, can cast long shadows over current behavior, influencing how you perceive and interact with others. By analyzing these impacts, you gain awareness and control, breaking free from cycles that no longer serve you.

In relationships, emotional awareness transforms communication and reduces misunderstandings. Integrating "I feel" statements into conversations allows you to express emotions clearly without assigning blame, fostering open dialogue and mutual understanding. For example, saying, "I feel upset when plans change unexpectedly," communicates your feelings without criticism, paving the way for constructive conversation. Active listening further enhances this process by fully focusing on your partner's words and emotions, demonstrating empathy and respect. This practice encourages deeper connections and resolves conflicts by addressing the underlying emotions.

Setting aside time for regular emotional check-ins with loved ones strengthens bonds and keeps relationships healthy. These moments of reflection, where both parties share and listen, build trust and understanding. They offer a safe space to discuss emotions and address concerns before they escalate, promoting a harmonious and supportive environment. Emotional check-ins also allow one to celebrate successes and navigate challenges together, reinforcing the partnership's resilience. In the next chapter, we will explore the nuances of emotional manipulation, examining how awareness can defend against such tactics.

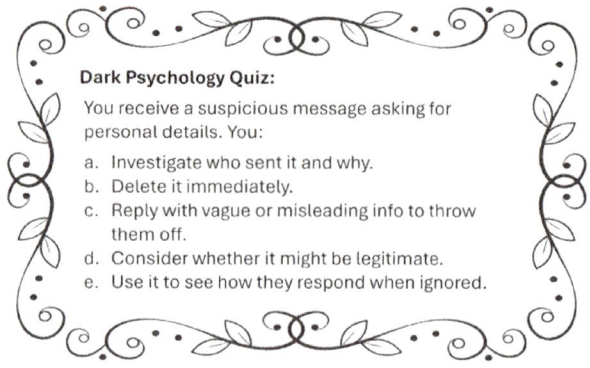

Dark Psychology Quiz:

You receive a suspicious message asking for personal details. You:

a. Investigate who sent it and why.
b. Delete it immediately.
c. Reply with vague or misleading info to throw them off.
d. Consider whether it might be legitimate.
e. Use it to see how they respond when ignored.

Chapter 14: Identifying and Overcoming Pain Points

Understanding the roots of fear is the first step toward dismantling it. Often, this fear is cultivated by social conditioning, past experiences, and cultural norms that discourage assertiveness. Many are taught to prioritize harmony over conflict from a young age, leading to a reluctance to voice dissenting opinions. This conditioning is reinforced by the fear of rejection or disapproval, where the anticipation of adverse reactions from others can be paralyzing. Negative past experiences with confrontation can also leave an indelible mark, as memories of arguments gone awry or unresolved disputes haunt your willingness to engage in future confrontations. Cultural or familial norms may further compound this fear, particularly in environments where assertiveness is undervalued or misunderstood. In such contexts, confrontation is often equated with aggression, pushing you to silence your voice to maintain a superficial peace. Recognizing these underlying causes is essential to addressing the fear of confrontation, as it allows you to identify specific triggers and challenge the beliefs that sustain them.

The importance of healthy confrontation cannot be overstated. It serves as a powerful tool for strengthening communication and understanding within relationships. Addressing issues openly and honestly prevents resentment and unresolved conflict from festering beneath the surface. Healthy confrontation paves the way for mutual respect and trust, demonstrating a commitment to transparency and collaboration. When approached constructively, confrontation can lead to positive outcomes that enhance the quality of your interactions. It empowers you to set boundaries protecting your wellbeing, ensuring your needs and values are respected. This process fosters healthier relationships and cultivates personal growth and self-confidence. Embracing confrontation as a constructive force enables you to maintain authenticity and integrity in your personal and professional life.

Managing confrontation anxiety involves developing techniques that promote calmness and composure, even in the face of tension. Deep breathing exercises reduce physiological stress, activating the body's relaxation response and lowering heart rate. Focusing on slow, deliberate breaths can soothe your nervous system and regain control over your emotions. Visualization techniques offer another powerful tool for managing anxiety. Mentally rehearsing successful confrontations allows you to anticipate potential challenges and visualize positive outcomes. This practice builds confidence and prepares you to navigate difficult conversations with clarity and poise. Setting specific objectives for the conversation further enhances your ability to manage anxiety. By defining your goals and desired outcomes in advance, you establish a clear framework for the discussion, reducing uncertainty and focusing your efforts on achieving resolution. These techniques mitigate anxiety and empower you to approach confrontation with purpose and determination.

Engaging in constructive confrontation requires practical steps prioritizing clarity, respect, and mutual understanding. Preparing talking points and anticipated responses lets you articulate your perspective clearly and confidently. Organizing your thoughts in advance minimizes the risk of becoming sidetracked or overwhelmed during the conversation. Active listening plays a crucial role in validating the other person's perspective. You create an environment of openness and respect by fully engaging with their words and demonstrating empathy. This approach fosters mutual understanding and facilitates productive dialogue. Maintaining a calm and neutral tone throughout the discussion is equally important. It sets the tone for a respectful exchange and minimizes the likelihood of escalating tension. Following up with a summary of the agreed-upon points reinforces clarity and ensures that both parties are on the same page. This step consolidates the progress made during the conversation and lays the foundation for ongoing communication and cooperation.

Visualization for Confrontation

Take a moment to close your eyes and imagine a situation where you need to engage in confrontation. Visualize yourself confidently entering the conversation, clearly articulating your points, and actively listening to the other person. Picture the discussion unfolding smoothly, with both parties reaching an understanding. Focus on the positive emotions of successful resolution, such as relief and empowerment. This visualization exercise can help alleviate anxiety and prepare you for constructive confrontation.

By understanding the roots of fear, recognizing the value of healthy confrontation, and employing techniques to manage anxiety, you equip yourself with the skills necessary for effective communication. Embracing confrontation as an opportunity for growth and connection allows you to navigate relationships with confidence and integrity. Feel free to write any notes if they assist.

Building Confidence in Recognizing Manipulation

Recognizing manipulation is like learning a new rhythm in the intricate dance of human interactions. It requires attention to detail and the ability to perceive subtle shifts that might go unnoticed. Identifying manipulation patterns begins with noticing inconsistencies in stories or explanations. When someone frequently changes their account, it can signal deceit. Please pay attention to these discrepancies, which often indicate a deeper strategy. Similarly, excessive flattery or undue pressure should raise a flag. Compliments are standard in conversation, but when they seem exaggerated or are used to sway your decisions, they might be a tool for manipulation. An observant eye is also crucial for detecting body language changes when someone is questioned. A sudden shift in posture, avoidance of eye contact, or fidgeting can reveal discomfort or deceit. These physical cues are often more telling than words, providing insights into a person's true intentions.

Developing intuition and gut feelings is another essential skill in recognizing manipulation. Your subconscious often picks up on subtle cues before your conscious mind can articulate them. Trusting this internal radar can be invaluable. Reflect on past experiences where your intuition was correct. Remember times when you had a hunch about a person's intentions and how those situations unfolded? Acknowledging these moments can reinforce your trust in your instincts. Practicing mindfulness can enhance this present-moment awareness. By staying attuned to your thoughts and feelings, you become more adept at noticing when something feels off. Mindfulness allows you to tune into those gut feelings without immediate judgment, giving you the space to process what you're sensing. It encourages a deeper connection to your internal cues, making it easier to recognize manipulation before it escalates. The more you listen to your intuition, the more you reinforce its reliability.

Building self-assuredness and assertiveness is key to standing firm against manipulative tactics. Start by practicing assertive communication in low-stakes environments. Whether ordering a meal at a restaurant or expressing a preference in a group setting, these small exercises build confidence in voicing your needs. Over time, these skills transfer to more challenging situations, fortifying your ability to assert yourself when it counts. Setting personal affirmations can also reinforce your confidence. Positive self-talk, such as reminding yourself of your strengths and capabilities, bolsters your self-esteem and fortitude. These affirmations serve as a mental anchor, grounding you in your worth and helping you resist manipulation. By cultivating a strong sense of self, you create a protective shield against those seeking to exploit your vulnerabilities.

Utilizing support systems is a powerful strategy for validating your perceptions and reducing self-doubt. Feedback from trusted friends or mentors can provide an external perspective, offering clarity when your judgment feels clouded. These individuals can act as sounding boards, helping you process your experiences and confirming whether your concerns are valid. Joining groups focused on personal development and empowerment creates a support network where you can share experiences and learn from others. These communities foster growth and resilience, equipping you with the skills to navigate manipulative environments. Participating in workshops or seminars on communication skills further enhances your ability to stand up against manipulation. These settings provide practical tools and strategies, enabling you to refine your assertiveness in a supportive environment. The synergy of a strong support network and continued personal development fortifies your defenses against manipulation, building a foundation of confidence and assurance.

As you strengthen your ability to recognize manipulation, remember that each step you take enhances your empowerment and resilience. Your growing awareness and confidence form a solid base from which you can engage with the world on your terms. With these skills, you're better equipped to navigate life's complexities, ensuring that your interactions are guided by authenticity and integrity. The journey of understanding and overcoming manipulation is a continuous process that will serve you well as you explore the realms of psychological warfare and defense strategies in the chapters ahead.

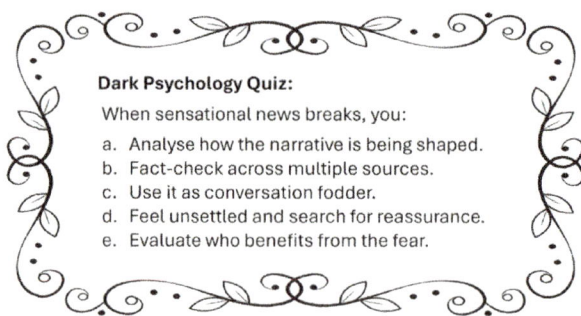

Dark Psychology Quiz:

When sensational news breaks, you:
a. Analyse how the narrative is being shaped.
b. Fact-check across multiple sources.
c. Use it as conversation fodder.
d. Feel unsettled and search for reassurance.
e. Evaluate who benefits from the fear.

Chapter 15: Tools for Better Relationships

Communicating effectively in challenging situations requires more than words; it demands understanding the intricate dance between emotion and dialogue. Difficult conversations often trigger a cascade of emotions, which can cloud judgment and escalate tensions if not managed with care.

Understanding the dynamics of these conversations involves recognizing the emotional triggers that may arise. Timing is crucial; initiating a discussion when emotions run high can lead to unproductive exchanges. Choosing a moment when both parties are calm and receptive is essential, allowing for a more constructive interaction. Setting plays a significant role as well. Opt for a neutral environment that minimizes distractions and fosters a sense of safety. This could be a quiet room where you can speak freely, away from the pressures of everyday life. Creating a conducive atmosphere helps ease tension, allowing for more open and honest communication.

Active listening forms the bedrock of effective communication. It involves more than just hearing words; it requires a deliberate effort to understand the speaker's message fully. By practicing active listening, you demonstrate respect and empathy, ensuring the other person feels valued and understood. Techniques such as paraphrasing the speaker's words can confirm your comprehension, signaling that you are engaged and attentive. You might say, "So, what I hear you saying is..." to reflect on their message, providing an opportunity for clarification. Non-verbal cues like nodding and maintaining eye contact reinforce your attentiveness, creating a sense of connection. Avoiding interruptions is equally vital, allowing the speaker to express themselves fully without feeling rushed or undermined. By embracing these techniques, you lay the groundwork for a dialogue that is both respectful and productive.

Using "I" statements is a powerful tool in navigating difficult conversations. This approach shifts the focus from blame to personal experience, reducing defensiveness and promoting openness. By framing your feelings with "I" statements, you express your emotions and needs without assigning blame or criticism. For instance, instead of saying, "You never listen to me," you might express, "I feel frustrated when I don't feel heard because it makes me feel unimportant." This subtle shift in language fosters a more collaborative atmosphere, inviting the other person to engage without feeling attacked. Practicing with specific scenarios can build confidence, allowing you to articulate your thoughts clearly and constructively.

This technique enhances communication and strengthens the foundation of trust and understanding within your relationships.

In moments when emotions threaten to derail a conversation, de-escalation techniques can help maintain a constructive dialogue. Taking breaks can provide the space needed to regain composure and perspective if tensions rise. Stepping away for a few moments allows both parties to cool down, preventing the escalation of conflict. Breathing exercises are another effective tool, as they promote relaxation and clarity of thought. Deep, measured breaths can soothe the nervous system, helping you stay calm and focused. Reframing negative language into neutral terms can also defuse tension, shifting the tone of the conversation from adversarial to collaborative. Choosing non-confrontational words creates an environment where solutions can emerge organically, fostering a sense of mutual respect and understanding.

Fostering Genuine Connections

Authenticity is the cornerstone of meaningful relationships, inviting others to engage with us honestly and transparently. Being true to oneself is not merely about expressing opinions or preferences; it involves embracing one's full range of emotions, strengths, and vulnerabilities. This openness encourages others to reciprocate, creating a space where genuine connections can flourish. Sharing personal stories and experiences is a powerful way to build rapport, as it reveals the fabric of who you are and fosters an environment of trust and understanding. When you open up about your triumphs and struggles, you signal that you value honesty over pretense, inviting others to share their narratives. However, authenticity does not mean abandoning all boundaries. It's about balancing being open and protecting your personal space, ensuring your interactions remain healthy and respectful.

Building trust and reliability in relationships requires consistent effort and integrity. Keeping promises and fulfilling commitments are fundamental practices that solidify trust. When you follow through on your word, you demonstrate reliability, reassuring others that they can depend on you. Consistency is key; showing up and being present in momentous and mundane times reinforces this trust. It signals that the relationship holds importance and that you are invested in nurturing it. Transparency in intentions and actions further strengthens this bond. By openly communicating your thoughts and intentions, you eliminate ambiguity. This transparency allows for clearer understanding and smoother interactions as both parties align their expectations and goals.

Cultivating empathy and understanding is indispensable to connect with others on a deeper level. Empathy involves more than simply sympathizing; it's about genuinely stepping into another's shoes to experience their perspective. Practicing perspective-taking can enhance your ability to see situations from others' viewpoints, fostering empathy and reducing misunderstandings. This approach enables you to respond with greater compassion and insight as you become attuned to the emotions and motivations driving others' actions. Engaging in empathy exercises, such as role-playing, can also be beneficial. These exercises allow you to practice responding to various scenarios with empathy, honing your ability to connect with others emotionally. By cultivating empathy, you enrich your relationships and create an environment where understanding and support become the norm.

Shared interests and activities are powerful catalysts for nurturing relationships, providing common ground and mutual enjoyment. Participating in clubs or groups centered around shared hobbies offers opportunities to connect with others who share similar passions. Whether it's a book club, a hiking group, or a cooking class, these settings provide a relaxed atmosphere where genuine connections can blossom naturally. Planning regular activities or outings based on mutual interests further strengthens these bonds. It could be as simple as a monthly movie night or a weekend brunch, where the focus is on enjoying each other's company and creating shared memories. Establishing traditions or rituals within these relationships can also contribute to their longevity. Whether it's an annual trip or a holiday gathering, these rituals serve as touchstones, reminding you of the value and continuity of the relationship.

As we navigate the complexities of building and maintaining authentic connections, it's essential to remember that the effort invested in fostering these relationships pays dividends in the form of deeper understanding, trust, and mutual support.

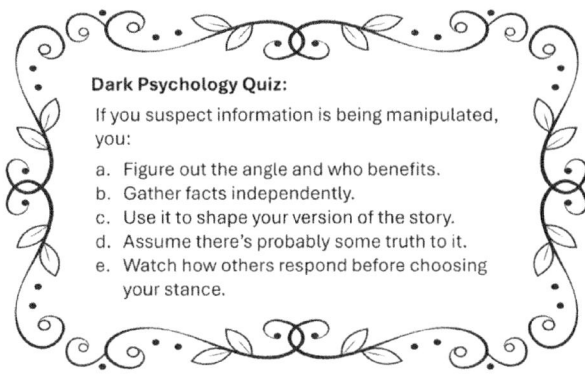

Dark Psychology Quiz:

If you suspect information is being manipulated, you:

a. Figure out the angle and who benefits.
b. Gather facts independently.
c. Use it to shape your version of the story.
d. Assume there's probably some truth to it.
e. Watch how others respond before choosing your stance.

Chapter 16: Recognizing Manipulation in Media

Like many forms of media, movies wield the subtle power of propaganda, a tool used throughout history to shape public perception and behavior. Propaganda, at its core, is a deliberate and systematic effort to manipulate perceptions, often adopting various media forms to achieve its goals. From the grandiose posters of wartime campaigns to the sleek advertisements that populate our daily lives, propaganda seeks to influence and direct actions that serve specific interests.

Historically, propaganda has played a significant role in shaping societal narratives, particularly during times of conflict. During World War II, propaganda was a powerful weapon the Axis and Allied forces wielded. Adolf Hitler employed a vast array of media - from films to music - to champion Nazi ideology while suppressing opposition. The propaganda not only glorified the German military might but also demonized Allied forces, influencing public sentiment and morale. Similarly, the British and Americans launched their own campaigns to galvanize public support and morale. Posters and films boosted wartime production, instilling a sense of duty and urgency among citizens. These historical examples underscore the pervasive influence of propaganda in rallying nations and manipulating collective emotions.

Fast forward to the present, and propaganda remains a staple in modern political campaigns and commercial advertising. Political campaigns craft narratives that appeal to emotions and values, often employing strategies that echo historical techniques. The bandwagon approach, for instance, suggests that everyone supports a particular candidate or cause, nudging you to conform. This technique preys on the natural human desire to belong, subtly pressuring individuals to align with perceived majority opinions. In advertising, glittering generalities employ vague yet emotionally charged language to evoke positive feelings without providing concrete evidence. Phrases like "new and improved" or "best in class" promise benefits while remaining ambiguous. The transfer technique, another common tactic, associates a product or idea with a positive image or emotion, such as happiness, success, or patriotism. Advertisers create an emotional connection that transcends logical analysis by linking these emotions to a brand.

The testimonial approach leverages endorsements from celebrities or experts to lend credibility and influence consumer decisions. When a trusted figure advocates for a product or cause, audiences are more likely to accept the message as valid. Fear tactics, on the other hand, exploit anxieties and insecurities to drive action. Advertisements that suggest dire consequences for not using a product tap into a primal fear response, compelling you to act out of concern for your wellbeing. These techniques, while varied, share a common goal: to influence behavior by appealing to emotions and instincts rather than rational thought.

To navigate this landscape, it's crucial to develop the ability to analyze visual and verbal cues in propaganda. For example, color symbolism in political posters can evoke specific emotions and associations. Red often signifies urgency or power, while blue might convey calm and trust. These intentional color choices elicit subconscious responses that align with the propagandist's objectives. In propaganda videos, music and sound are pivotal in setting the tone and enhancing emotional impact. A triumphant score can inspire pride and unity, while a somber melody may underscore themes of sacrifice or urgency. The language used in speeches or advertisements often contains loaded words and emotional language crafted to provoke strong reactions. By recognizing these elements, you can unravel the emotional manipulation at play.

Media and Critical Thinking

Consider the role of propaganda in environmental campaigns, where imagery and messaging are used to sway public opinion on climate change and conservation efforts. Campaigns often employ emotionally charged visuals of natural beauty juxtaposed with images of destruction, compelling audiences to act in defence of the planet. These campaigns harness the power of fear tactics, suggesting dire consequences if action is not taken. They also use testimonials from respected scientists and environmentalists to lend authority to their message. In historical revolutions, propaganda has catalyzed change, rallying the masses against oppressive regimes. From pamphlets and posters to speeches and songs, these movements utilized propaganda to unify disparate groups under a common cause, shaping cultural narratives and societal values.

In today's media-saturated environment, propaganda influences cultural narratives, reinforcing stereotypes or promoting specific ideologies. Whether through films, news outlets, or social media, these narratives shape how we perceive the world and our place within it. Understanding the mechanisms of propaganda empowers you to critically assess the media you consume, fostering a more informed and discerning perspective. By recognizing the techniques employed to sway opinions, you can confidently navigate the media landscape, ensuring your beliefs and decisions are yours.

Navigating the digital landscape today feels like being in a labyrinth of information, misinformation, and disinformation, where each day presents a new headline, a viral post, or a breaking news alert. The sheer volume of content on countless platforms can overwhelm even the most discerning reader. In this environment, media literacy becomes a skill and a necessity for empowerment. It allows you to sift through the noise, identify credible information, and make informed decisions. Media literacy is accessing, analyzing, evaluating, and creating media in various forms. By honing this skill, you gain the power to navigate the complex web of modern media, discerning fact from fiction and uncovering the motives behind the messages.

The proliferation of information sources, from traditional media to social media platforms, has dramatically altered how we consume and understand news. With so many voices competing for attention, it's easy to become lost in a sea of conflicting narratives and biased reporting. Media literacy enables you to cut through this clutter, empowering you to assess the information you encounter critically. This skill is vital not only for personal decision-making but also for democratic participation. Informed citizens are better equipped to engage in civic activities, make educated voting choices, and hold leaders accountable. Recognizing bias and propaganda in media content helps protect democratic processes from manipulation, ensuring that public discourse remains grounded in reality rather than misinformation.

Developing critical thinking skills is essential for navigating the media landscape. These skills enable you to question the information presented, evaluate its credibility, and recognize underlying biases. Start by differentiating between fact and opinion in news articles. Facts are verifiable truths, while opinions are interpretations or judgments. News articles often blend the two, so look for phrases that signal opinions, such as "experts believe" or "critics argue." Next, evaluate the credibility of sources and authors. Consider the publication's reputation, the author's expertise, and any potential conflicts of interest. Reliable sources typically provide evidence and cite their information. Recognizing bias in media reporting is another crucial aspect. Bias can manifest in the selection of topics, the framing of issues, and the language used. Pay attention to whether multiple perspectives are presented and if the coverage seems balanced or skewed.

To enhance your media literacy, take advantage of various tools and resources designed to help you critically evaluate media content. Fact-checking websites and apps, such as Snopes and FactCheck.org, are invaluable for verifying the accuracy of information. These platforms investigate claims and provide evidence-based assessments of their validity. Educational programs and workshops on media literacy offer structured learning opportunities, equipping you with the skills to analyze media critically. Many institutions and organizations provide free or low-cost in-person and online courses to educate individuals on media literacy principles. Online courses focusing on critical media analysis further deepen your understanding of how media influences perceptions and behaviors, enabling you to apply these insights in everyday life.

Engaging in practical exercises can also foster a habit of critical media consumption. Start by analyzing a news story from multiple perspectives. Seek out different sources covering the same event, noting variations in tone, emphasis, and interpretation. This practice helps you identify bias and recognize the influence of editorial choices. Another helpful exercise is conducting a media diet, where you consciously reduce exposure to biased or sensationalist sources. By curating your media consumption, you can focus on more balanced and reputable outlets, improving the quality of information you receive. Participating in discussions and debates on current media topics further hone your critical thinking skills. Engaging with others challenges your perspectives and encourages you to articulate your views clearly and thoughtfully. Through these interactions, you gain new insights and refine your ability to evaluate media content critically.

Incorporating these practices into your daily routine strengthens your media literacy, empowering you to navigate the digital landscape with confidence and discernment. As you develop these skills, you become better equipped to engage with media critically, ensuring that reliable and diverse sources inform your understanding of the world. This awareness enhances decision-making and contributes to a more informed and engaged society.

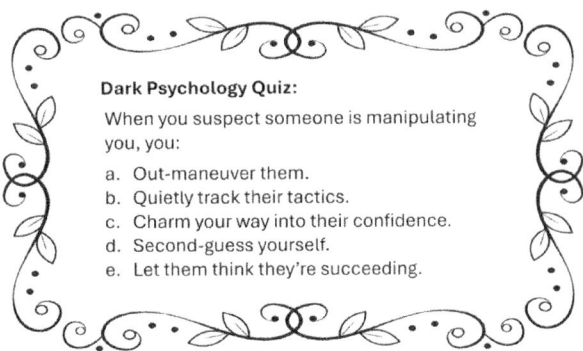

Dark Psychology Quiz:

When you suspect someone is manipulating you, you:

a. Out-maneuver them.
b. Quietly track their tactics.
c. Charm your way into their confidence.
d. Second-guess yourself.
e. Let them think they're succeeding.

Chapter 17: The Ethics of Influence

Persuasion and manipulation straddle a fine line, yet their differences are crucial. Persuasion thrives on transparency, respecting the autonomy of others while openly presenting facts and benefits. It relies on mutual understanding and cooperation, where the persuader respects the audience's decision-making process. The objective is not to dominate but to inform, allowing individuals to make educated choices. On the other hand, manipulation cloaks its true intentions, often serving self-interest at the expense of others. It breaches trust, using deception to sway decisions, leaving little room for genuine choice. Manipulation employs emotional exploitation, fear, and misinformation to corner someone into compliance, often prioritizing the manipulator's gain over the wellbeing of the individual. A salesperson may use manipulation by exaggerating a product's features beyond their true capabilities. At the same time, an ethical counterpart would highlight its genuine benefits, allowing the customer to decide based on honest information.

The ethical principles underpinning persuasion emphasize honesty, transparency, and respect for autonomy. Honesty means accurately presenting information, avoiding exaggeration, and substantiating claims. This builds trust and credibility, which is essential for maintaining long-term relationships. Transparency involves communicating intentions and goals, ensuring that the audience understands the purpose behind the interaction. It means being open about potential conflicts of interest and allowing individuals to see the whole picture before deciding. Respecting autonomy is the most critical aspect, acknowledging that everyone can make their own choices without undue influence. It involves encouraging informed decision-making, where the audience feels empowered and respected rather than coerced. In contrast, manipulation often disregards these principles, employing tactics that undermine autonomy and erode trust.

Recognizing manipulative tactics is key to protecting oneself from deceptive influence. Emotional exploitation, such as guilt-tripping or fear-mongering, is common in manipulation. It plays on insecurities and vulnerabilities, compelling individuals to act out of anxiety or obligation rather than genuine interest. Manipulators may withhold important information or distort facts, creating a skewed reality that pressures you into compliance. False urgency is another tactic where you are made to believe that immediate action is necessary, often leading to rushed decisions that benefit the manipulator. Understanding these tactics allows you to discern when a situation shifts from persuasion to manipulation, empowering you to maintain control over your choices.

Consider an advertising campaign that misleads by promoting a product as a miracle cure without scientific backing. Such a campaign manipulates by exploiting fears and offering false hope, ultimately damaging trust and credibility. In contrast, an honest awareness campaign that educates the public about the benefits of a product, supported by research and transparent data, fosters informed decision-making and builds trust. Political campaigns often use fear to manipulate voters, presenting exaggerated threats to influence choices. Ethical campaigns, however, focus on informed choice, presenting clear policies, and allowing voters to decide based on a comprehensive understanding of the issues.

Identifying Influence Tactics

Reflect on a recent advertisement or social media post that caught your attention. Was the message clear and based on evidence, or did it use exaggerated claims and urgency? Please write down your thoughts and identify whether they leaned more towards persuasion or manipulation. Consider how this knowledge impacts your perception of the message and decision-making process.

Understanding the ethics of influence is crucial in navigating the complex landscape of human interactions. You can make informed choices and maintain autonomy by recognizing the fine line between persuasion and manipulation. Whether you're facing a savvy marketer or a persuasive friend, these insights equip you to engage with confidence and clarity.

Ethical Influence in Everyday Life

In personal relationships, ethical influence is not just about the words you choose; it's about fostering environments where trust and mutual respect thrive. Picture a close friendship where you want to encourage your friend to adopt healthier habits. Instead of pressuring them with ultimatums, share your experiences of how a morning walk has positively impacted your mood and energy levels. This approach is more effective because it comes from shared understanding and encouragement rather than coercion. Positive reinforcement plays a crucial role here - you celebrate small milestones together, perhaps by acknowledging each other's progress over a cup of tea. This method encourages change and strengthens your bond, respecting their autonomy and choice.

Ethical influence becomes a cornerstone of effective leadership and teamwork in professional settings. Consider a manager who leads by example, setting a tone of integrity and transparency within the team.

They present clear goals, provide the necessary support, and encourage open communication, fostering an environment where team members feel valued and empowered to contribute. This manager understands that ethical influence is not about wielding power over others but inspiring them to achieve their best. The manager creates a mutual respect and trust culture by fostering collaboration and acknowledging each team member's strengths. In such a setting, employees are more engaged, motivated, and likely to share innovative ideas, knowing their contributions are appreciated and respected.

Transitioning to marketing and advertising, ethical influence takes on a different yet equally important role. Imagine a brand that prides itself on transparent sustainability practices. Instead of making vague claims, it provides clear and accurate product information, detailing the steps to ensure environmentally friendly sourcing and production. This transparency builds trust with consumers, who feel confident supporting a brand aligning with their values. The brand attracts a loyal customer base by engaging with customers through honest communication. It sets a standard for ethical practices within the industry. This approach is supported by a case study where a brand's commitment to transparency and sustainability led to increased consumer trust and loyalty.

Balancing influence with consent is another key aspect of ethical influence. This means ensuring individuals retain their freedom of choice in any persuasive endeavor. Take, for instance, a financial advisor who presents a range of investment options to a client. Instead of pushing a specific product, they provide all the relevant information, allowing the client to make an informed decision. The advisor seeks explicit consent, ensuring clients feel comfortable and confident in their choices. This method respects the client's autonomy and reinforces trust in the advisor-client relationship. By encouraging informed decisions without pressure, ethical influence empowers individuals to take control of their choices, fostering a sense of confidence and independence.

Understanding these principles of ethical influence can transform how you interact with others, whether in personal relationships, professional settings, or consumer interactions. By applying these practices, you create environments prioritizing trust, transparency, and mutual respect, paving the way for more authentic and meaningful connections. These insights also equip you with the tools to navigate complex situations with integrity, ensuring your influence remains practical and ethical. As you continue to explore the nuances of influence in various aspects of life, these principles will serve as a guiding framework, helping you engage with others in a way that honors their autonomy and respects their choices.

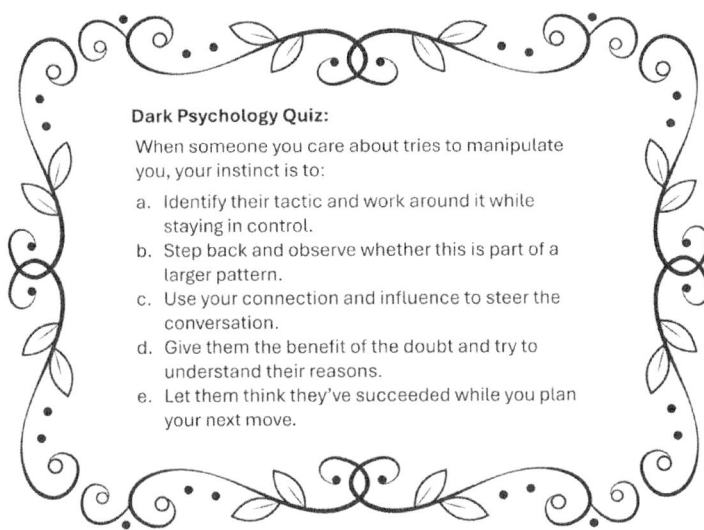

Dark Psychology Quiz:

When someone you care about tries to manipulate you, your instinct is to:

a. Identify their tactic and work around it while staying in control.
b. Step back and observe whether this is part of a larger pattern.
c. Use your connection and influence to steer the conversation.
d. Give them the benefit of the doubt and try to understand their reasons.
e. Let them think they've succeeded while you plan your next move.

Chapter 18: Confront a Manipulator Without Losing Power (Bonus Chapter)

When we think about confronting someone who has manipulated us, we often imagine it like a scene from a movie - dramatic, explosive, and final. We picture ourselves standing tall, calm and unshakable, while the other person is finally forced to see the truth, apologise, or at the very least, be exposed. It's a fantasy of justice that many of us hold close, especially when we've spent so long second-guessing ourselves or being made to feel like we're the problem.

But real confrontation, especially with someone who uses manipulation, rarely looks like that. It's not always loud. It doesn't always end with clarity or closure. In fact, it often leaves the manipulator unchanged - and you, emotionally drained. And that's why it's important to shift how we define confrontation altogether.

True confrontation isn't about winning. It isn't about proving your point so perfectly that the other person has no choice but to admit fault. It's not about having the last word or seeing a dramatic shift in their behaviour. Instead, it's about something much quieter - and much more powerful. It's about expressing yourself with clarity. It's about holding your boundary, whether they respect it or not. And it's about walking away with your dignity, your peace, and your sense of self intact.

It's also important to acknowledge something that doesn't get said enough: not every manipulator can or should be confronted. In some cases, the risk is too high. The fallout too heavy. The person too unwilling to listen or reflect. And that doesn't mean you're weak. It doesn't mean you've failed to stand up for yourself. Choosing not to confront someone can be a sign of immense wisdom and strength - because you're prioritising your energy, your safety, and your future.

This chapter isn't about gearing you up for a battle. It's here to help you decide if a confrontation is right for you - and if it is, how to do it in a way that protects your power rather than costs you it. Whether you speak your truth in a conversation or simply in a journal, the act of reclaiming your clarity is confrontation enough. And you get to define what that looks like.

Preparation is Power

Before confronting someone who has manipulated you, the most powerful thing you can do is pause - not to avoid the moment, but to prepare for it. Confrontation isn't something that has to happen in the heat of the moment, or when your emotions are at their peak. In fact, the more intentional and grounded you are, the more likely you are to walk away feeling clear, not scrambled.

Start by getting grounded - emotionally and physically. This means slowing down enough to understand what's happening in your body and your mind. Are you feeling tight in your chest? Shaky in your hands? Cloudy in your thinking? Those are all signs that your nervous system is on high alert, and it may not be the best moment to speak yet. Take a walk. Breathe deeply. Place your feet flat on the floor. Do whatever helps you come back to yourself before stepping into the conversation. You don't need to feel totally calm, but you do need to feel present.

Next, get clear on your why. Are you hoping to name harm that's been done, set a new boundary, or ask for a change in behaviour? Each of those goals requires a slightly different approach and knowing what yours is will help you stay focused - especially if the conversation starts to go sideways. This is the heart of your confrontation: what you're doing it for, and what you're not. For example, if your goal is to reclaim your voice and express what hurt you, you don't need the other person to admit they were wrong for it to be valid. If your goal is to set a boundary, their agreement isn't necessary - your clarity is.

It's also vital to prepare for pushback. Manipulative people often respond with defensiveness, deflection, or even false charm. They might try to twist your words, change the subject, or make you feel like the problem. Expect this. Not so you're cynical - but so you're ready. Knowing how they might respond gives you the chance to plan how you will stay steady. You can write out phrases you'll repeat if they interrupt. You can rehearse your tone or even jot down notes to read from during the conversation if needed. This isn't weakness - it's strategy.

One powerful preparation tool is journaling. Try asking yourself:
- "What am I expecting them to say?"
- "How can I stay calm even if they react badly?"
- "What would 'success' look like for me in this confrontation?"

You can also use self-talk scripts, spoken aloud or written down, to strengthen your internal voice. For example:
- "I'm allowed to say this."
- "I'm not responsible for how they take it."
- "I can end the conversation if I feel unsafe."

Preparation doesn't guarantee the conversation will go well - but it does mean that no matter how it unfolds, you'll know what you came there to say. That's the part you can control. And that's the part that restores your power.

Words That Hold Power

When you're confronting someone who uses manipulation, the words you choose matter - not just for them, but for you. Clear, direct language is a kind of armour. It doesn't need to be loud, dramatic, or emotionally charged. In fact, the most powerful language in these moments is often calm, concise, and emotionally grounded.

The goal is to speak in a way that is difficult to twist or deflect. Manipulators are often skilled at taking vague language and bending it, reframing it, or pretending not to understand. So instead of using soft qualifiers or emotional explanations they can pick apart - like "I just feel like maybe you were kind of being unfair..." - we speak with clarity and intention. We name what happened, how it impacted us, and what we will no longer accept.

Here's a basic but effective formula to follow:
"When X happened, I felt Y. I won't allow that again."

This structure does three things: it keeps you focused on facts and feelings, it removes room for argument, and it draws a clear line. You're not accusing them of being a terrible person, you're naming a behaviour and owning its impact on you - then making your boundary clear.

Let's break that formula into four essential parts:

1. **Name the Behaviour**

Start by stating what happened, specifically and plainly. Avoid using dramatic or charged language, and focus on actions, not character. Instead of "You always try to control me," say:

"When you gave me the silent treatment after I set a boundary..."

This grounds the conversation in something real and observable. It's harder to argue with a described action than with a sweeping generalisation.

2. **State the Impact**

Next, explain how that behaviour affected you. Use I language here - not to soften the blow, but to centre your own reality.

"...I felt isolated and anxious. I started questioning whether I was allowed to say no."

You're not asking them to validate your emotions - you're claiming them. You're also helping them understand that their behaviour has a cost.

3. **Set the Limit**

This is where your boundary becomes visible. It might be a firm refusal, a line in the sand, or a description of what won't continue.
"That behaviour isn't okay with me. I need it to stop."
The point here isn't to persuade them. It's to inform them of the new terms of engagement - ones that protect your wellbeing.

4. **End the Loop**

Manipulators thrive on circular conversations. They'll deflect, change the subject, question your tone, or push you to justify everything you've said. That's why you need an end point. Something that says: "We're not looping this endlessly."
You can say:
"This isn't a debate. I've said what I needed to say."
This is where you reclaim your exit. You're not there to win an argument. You're there to honour your clarity. Once that's done, you're allowed to walk away - whether they understand you or not.
Some other powerful phrases to consider using:
- "I'm not here to argue - I'm here to make my boundary clear."
- "I've thought carefully about this. My decision isn't open for negotiation."
- "I'm not continuing this conversation if it keeps going in circles."

The key takeaway? You are allowed to say something once. You are allowed to say it quietly. You are allowed to say it and then leave.
Clarity is strength. You don't have to convince anyone - you just have to mean it.

Staying Grounded in the Moment

Confronting someone who has manipulated you is rarely just a mental challenge - it's a physical one. Our bodies remember what it feels like to be on unstable ground. They hold the history of conversations that made us feel small, confused, dismissed or gaslit. So even when you walk into a confrontation well-prepared and clear on your words, your nervous system may still react.
It's important to know that these reactions are normal. You might feel your heart racing, your hands trembling, or your stomach tightening. You might go blank, lose your train of thought, or feel frozen in place - unable to speak. This is your body slipping into a protective state, like fight, flight or freeze. It's not a sign that you're weak. It's a sign that your body is trying

to keep you safe.

The trick isn't to force yourself to be perfectly composed - it's to anchor yourself while you move through the discomfort. And you can do that using simple, intentional techniques to help bring your nervous system back into balance in real time.

Start with your breath. When we're panicked, our breath becomes shallow and fast, which fuels the anxiety loop. Try box breathing: inhale for a count of four, hold for four, exhale for four, and pause for four. Do this for just one or two rounds - it can help calm your heart rate and return focus to your body.

Another simple grounding gesture is placing your hand over your chest - the physical pressure and warmth can bring a sense of reassurance. If that doesn't feel good for you, try pressing your feet into the floor and becoming aware of your connection to the ground beneath you. Stability isn't just mental - it's physical, too.

In the moment, you can also repeat a quiet mantra in your mind, especially if the other person starts to deflect, interrupt or emotionally escalate. Try phrases like:

- "I am calm. I am clear. I am safe."
- "I don't need to win this. I just need to hold my boundary."
- "I can leave at any time."

These grounding phrases give your mind something solid to hold on to - a kind of inner handrail when things start to feel shaky.

And perhaps most importantly, remind yourself: you don't need them to be calm in order for you to stay calm. Manipulators often try to unbalance you through tone, pace, silence, or emotional escalation. They may raise their voice, change the subject, or start crying to draw the focus away from what you're saying. You don't have to absorb their chaos.

Don't chase calm in them - protect calm in you.

It is a radical act to hold your centre in a conversation designed to pull you off it. But with practice, and compassion for your body's responses, it becomes possible. Even if your voice shakes. Even if your heart pounds. You're allowed to speak and stay grounded - at the same time.

What Happens Next

You did it - you said the thing. You confronted the manipulator. You named the behaviour, stood your ground, and expressed your boundary. You walked in prepared, stayed as grounded as you could, and used your voice with intention. That alone is huge. But what happens next can be just as emotionally loaded as the confrontation itself - because the aftermath isn't always what we hope for.

Ideally, they'd respond with understanding, self-awareness, or even accountability. But manipulation doesn't dissolve just because it's been called out. And many manipulators don't react with openness - they react with defence.

Here are a few common behaviours to be ready for:

Gaslighting or Minimising

You might hear things like:
- "That's not what happened."
- "You're exaggerating."
- "I think you're being really unfair right now."

These phrases are designed to make you question your memory or feelings - often just when you've finally gathered the courage to name them. It can be deeply disorienting. You might feel yourself shrinking, retreating, wondering if you were too harsh. Stop there. Breathe. Remind yourself: you don't need permission to name harm.

Sudden Over-Apologies

In some cases, the person may swing in the opposite direction - offering a flood of apologies, tears, and dramatic regret.
- "I'm the worst. I mess everything up."
- "I can't believe I did that. Please don't hate me."

While this might look like accountability, it's often a tactic to refocus the emotional spotlight. Instead of addressing what you said, they create a new narrative - one where you feel compelled to comfort them. It's subtle, but effective. And it derails your boundary.

You can acknowledge the apology without collapsing into emotional caretaking. For example:

"Thank you for saying that. I still need space right now."
"I hear you, and I meant what I said."

Stonewalling or Coldness

Another common response is silence. Distance. Withholding. A manipulator may go quiet for hours or days, disappear from communication, or give clipped, emotionless responses. This is not maturity - it's control. It's a way to punish you for disrupting the dynamic.

But their withdrawal is not your responsibility. You set a boundary, not a bomb. Their discomfort belongs to them.

A Few Important Reminders

- Their reaction does not define the validity of your boundary. Whether they lash out, cry, ignore you, or try to guilt you - it doesn't change what you experienced. Your boundary is still valid. Your words are still true. You do not need their agreement for it to matter.
- You do not owe more explaining.
  You don't need to go back in, soften your point, or rework it into something more digestible. You said what you needed to say. That's enough. You're allowed to stop talking.
- Clarity is not cruelty.
  It's self-respect. And sometimes, that's all you walk away with - your own self-respect, intact. But that's more than enough.

The aftermath may be messy. But so is growth. Stay close to your centre. Journal what happened. Talk to someone you trust. Rest. You've already done the hardest part - you faced it. You showed up for yourself.

And that's the kind of strength that lasts.

When Confrontation Isn't Safe

It's a powerful thing to speak your truth. But it's also powerful to choose not to. In some situations, confrontation isn't safe - emotionally, physically, or psychologically. That doesn't make you weak. It doesn't mean you're avoiding growth or "letting them win." It means you're honouring your intuition. And that is the deepest form of self-protection there is.

Before you confront someone who has manipulated you, it's important to check in with your safety. Ask yourself:
- If this person has a history of lashing out, what might happen?
- Have they responded with threats, aggression, or intimidation in the past?
- Do I have support if this goes badly?
- Do I feel physically safe in their presence?

Even if the person doesn't pose a physical threat, you also need to check in with your emotional safety. Are you in a place where you could handle being gaslit, blamed, or made to feel small again? Are you resourced enough to manage the emotional fallout if they react badly? Are you doing this because you want clarity - or because you're still hoping they'll finally validate you?

If there's any doubt, pause. You don't have to walk into a confrontation simply because you want justice or closure. Sometimes, the closure is you choosing not to engage.

Instead of direct confrontation, there are other powerful - and quieter - ways to protect yourself.

Non-verbal boundaries are just as valid:

- You can reduce how often you respond to them.
- You can stop offering explanations or emotional labour.
- You can remove them from your social media or block their access to your space.
- You can shift from over-sharing to silence, from availability to absence.
- You can simply walk away - no declaration, no scene, no final "I deserve better" speech.

And that, too, is confrontation. Because it disrupts the dynamic. It says, "I will no longer play this role for you." You do not need to be witnessed to be powerful.

Sometimes the bravest thing you can do is choose yourself - silently, consistently, and without needing the manipulator to understand or approve.

You don't need their permission to protect your peace. You don't need a moment of cinematic clarity. You just need to believe that you're allowed to live without chaos.

And you are.

Holding Power Quietly

We grow up being told that strength looks like standing face to face with someone, unshaken, delivering the perfect words at the perfect time. But in reality, true strength doesn't always look like confrontation. Sometimes, it looks like knowing when to speak and when to step away. It looks like choosing silence not from fear, but from self-trust. It looks like no longer needing someone to see your side in order for you to believe it.

The most radical thing you can do - especially if you've been manipulated, gaslit, or made to feel small - is to stop performing for other people's understanding. You do not need to be fully understood to be valid. You do not need someone to agree with your experience in order for it to be real. You are allowed to walk away without the full stop, without the closure, without the final line.

That's what it means to hold power quietly. You are not less brave because you didn't scream. You are not less clear because you stammered. You are not less right because someone tried to twist your words. You do not have to make someone understand you. You only have to honour yourself.Again and again, in all the small moments that follow.

Final Thought

Take a moment for yourself now. Write one sentence you'd say - or wish you had said - if nothing stood in your way. This sentence doesn't need to be shared. It doesn't need to be perfect. It just needs to be yours. Say it. Read it aloud. Let it land. That's your voice.

Let it stay strong.

Chapter 19: Cultural Perspectives on Manipulation

Cultural norms and values determine how manipulation is perceived and accepted. In collectivist societies, where the group's wellbeing often takes precedence over individual desires, manipulation may be cloaked in the guise of preserving harmony. For instance, individuals might use indirect methods to influence decisions, framing their actions as beneficial for the community. This indirect approach is often subtle, relying on the shared understanding and implied meanings inherent in high-context communication. In contrast, individualistic cultures, which prioritize personal autonomy and direct expression, might experience manipulation as more explicit and overt. Here, manipulation can be linked to personal ambition and the pursuit of individual success, often seen in competitive environments where assertiveness is valued.

Communication styles play a significant role in how manipulation is executed and interpreted. High-context cultures, prevalent in many Asian and Middle Eastern societies, rely heavily on non-verbal cues and implicit messaging. In these settings, much of the communication is unspoken, requiring a shared cultural knowledge to interpret the underlying meanings. This can obscure manipulative intent, as messages are conveyed through gestures, tone, and context rather than direct words. On the other hand, low-context cultures, such as those in Western societies, favor explicit and direct communication. Here, words carry the primary message, making manipulative tactics more apparent and often easier to identify. The contrast between these styles can lead to misunderstandings, as one culture views it as subtlety. At the same time, another might perceive it as evasiveness.

The perception of authority and hierarchy further influences manipulation tactics, shaped by cultural attitudes toward power and leadership. In high power distance cultures, like those in parts of Asia, there is a strong respect for hierarchy and authority. This respect can prevent individuals from questioning those in power, enabling leaders to employ manipulative tactics without fear of challenge. For instance, a manager might use their position to subtly pressure employees into compliance, framing it as respect for authority. In contrast, Western cultures, which often exhibit low power distance, encourage questioning authority and valuing equality. Here, manipulation might require more sophisticated tactics, as individuals are more likely to challenge directives that appear self-serving or unethical.

Cultural Manipulation and Cultural Sensitivity

In a Middle Eastern family, the cultural norm of elder respect can be both a source of wisdom and a potential avenue for manipulation. Picture a scenario where an elderly family member uses their respected status to influence financial decisions, framing their advice as beneficial for the family's honor. This manipulation, though subtle, leverages cultural values to achieve personal financial gain, highlighting how deeply ingrained norms can obscure intent. Similarly, in a Japanese corporation, loyalty to the company is paramount. Here, manipulation might manifest as a leader pressuring employees to work excessive hours, justifying it as a dedication to the company's success. This approach exploits the cultural value of loyalty, using it as a tool to achieve corporate goals.

Understanding these cultural nuances is crucial for navigating global interactions, as they influence how manipulation is perceived and enacted. Recognizing the underlying values and communication styles allows a more nuanced understanding of manipulation's role in various societies. By acknowledging these differences, individuals can develop more effective strategies for recognizing and responding to manipulation, fostering cross-cultural respect and understanding.

Cultural sensitivity is not just a buzzword; it's a vital skill in navigating a world rich with diverse traditions and values. Recognizing manipulation requires understanding these differences. For example, cultural taboos, which are deeply ingrained beliefs about what is socially unacceptable, can be exploited by manipulators to apply pressure or exert control. In some societies, breaking these taboos might bring shame not just to individuals but to entire families. Manipulators can use this fear to their advantage, coercing individuals into actions they might otherwise resist. Similarly, cultural rituals, which often carry significant emotional weight, can be misused. A manipulator might invoke a traditional ceremony or practice to validate their demands, knowing that refusal could be seen as disrespectful or rebellious. Understanding these nuances helps identify when culture is being used as a manipulation tool rather than a genuine expression of values.

Adapting strategies to recognize manipulation across different cultural contexts involves modifying your communication style to resonate with the cultural norms of the people you interact with. For instance, in a high-context culture, paying close attention to non-verbal cues and implied meanings becomes crucial. In these settings, the unspoken word carries as much weight as what is explicitly stated. Conversely, in low-context cultures, where directness is valued, being straightforward and transparent in your communication is key. Seeking out individuals who are well-versed in the cultural nuances of a particular group can provide invaluable insights. These people can help you navigate complex social landscapes, pointing out behaviors that might not be immediately apparent to an outsider.

Building culturally inclusive support networks is another critical step. Multicultural community groups offer a rich tapestry of perspectives, providing a space where you can learn from other's experiences and share your own. These groups encourage dialogue and foster an environment of mutual respect and understanding. Consulting with culturally knowledgeable friends or colleagues can also be beneficial. These individuals can offer guidance and advice based on their experiences, helping you develop effective and culturally appropriate strategies. Creating safe cultural dialogue and learning spaces within your community or workplace can further enhance understanding. These spaces allow for open conversations about cultural differences and manipulation, promoting an environment where everyone feels valued and heard.

Embracing cultural sensitivity equips you with the tools to identify and counteract manipulation more effectively in our interconnected world. As you continue to explore the complexities of human behavior, consider how these insights into cultural dynamics can enrich your understanding of manipulation and influence.

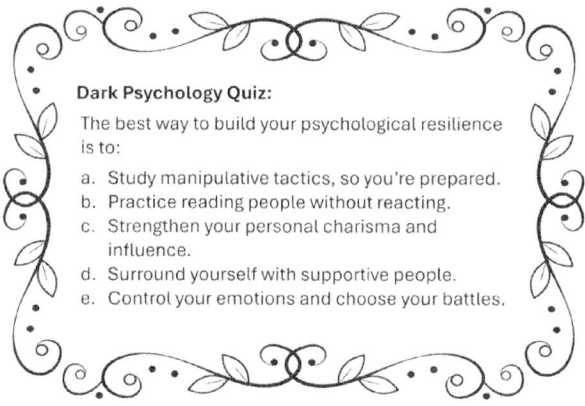

Dark Psychology Quiz:

The best way to build your psychological resilience is to:

a. Study manipulative tactics, so you're prepared.
b. Practice reading people without reacting.
c. Strengthen your personal charisma and influence.
d. Surround yourself with supportive people.
e. Control your emotions and choose your battles.

Chapter 20: Building a Supportive Community

Identifying and engaging with positive environments is crucial for developing a support network that champions open communication and mutual respect. Community centers, for instance, often offer support groups focused on emotional growth, providing a safe space for individuals to share experiences and learn from one another. These centers serve as a haven for personal development, where facilitators guide discussions on overcoming manipulation and building emotional intelligence.

In the digital age, online forums and social media groups dedicated to personal empowerment have become invaluable resources. They connect individuals with similar experiences, offering a platform for exchanging advice and support. These forums enable people to engage in meaningful conversations, regardless of geographical location, breaking down barriers that might otherwise limit access to community support. Additionally, local meet-ups focused on self-improvement and resilience provide opportunities for face-to-face interaction, fostering relationships that can be both empowering and enriching. Whether it's a book club discussing themes of empowerment or a workshop on emotional resilience, these gatherings offer a chance to connect with like-minded individuals committed to personal growth.

Shared experiences within a community are pivotal in building trust and understanding. They create a foundation for mutual support, where individuals feel seen and heard. Story-sharing sessions, for example, allow participants to connect emotionally, fostering empathy and solidarity. These sessions encourage openness and vulnerability, helping individuals process their experiences and gain new perspectives. Workshops that share personal journeys of overcoming manipulation further strengthen this bond, as they provide a platform for learning and growth. By listening to other's stories and sharing your own, you build resilience and contribute to a supportive network that uplifts and empowers its members.

Building such a personal network requires resources and strategies emphasizing inclusivity and accessibility. Local libraries often host community events and workshops, offering a space for individuals to come together and engage in activities that promote personal development. These events can range from mindfulness sessions to talks on setting boundaries and equipping attendees with tools to navigate life's challenges. Volunteer opportunities present another avenue for community building, allowing individuals to engage with diverse groups and contribute to causes that resonate with their values. Digital platforms, too, offer a wealth of resources for connecting with others. Whether through social media groups or dedicated websites, these platforms enable individuals to find communities that align with their interests and goals, fostering connections that transcend physical boundaries.

However, engaging with these supportive communities can sometimes be daunting, especially for those facing barriers such as social anxiety or lack of access. It's essential to recognize these challenges and develop strategies to overcome them. Gradually increasing social engagement can be effective, allowing individuals to build confidence and ease into community interactions. This might involve starting with small, manageable steps, such as attending a virtual meet-up or participating in an online discussion. For those with mobility constraints, online support options provide a valuable alternative, offering the same level of engagement and support as in-person events. Virtual meet-ups have become increasingly popular, providing a platform for individuals to connect without the pressure of physical attendance.

Community Engagement Checklist

Here's a Community Engagement Checklist for you to use. This will help you consciously build supportive, healthy connections, especially if you are recovering from manipulation or isolation. Use the note section below to record your thoughts.

1. **Identify your needs**
   - What type of support are you seeking? (Emotional, practical advice, accountability, shared interests)
   - Are you seeking peer support, expert guidance, or just social connection?
2. **Explore local resources**
   - Check community notice boards, libraries, and local councils for support groups, meet-ups, or classes.
   - Look for wellness or recovery groups focused on building resilience and emotional intelligence.
3. **Search for online forums and safe digital spaces**
   - Join forums or social media groups that align with your goals (e.g., parenting groups, mental health communities, professional networking).
   - Look for groups with clear guidelines around respect, safety, and privacy.
4. **Assess group culture before engaging**
   - Observe conversations before contributing.
   - Ask yourself: DOES THIS GROUP FEEL SUPPORTIVE OR

COMPETITIVE?
- Avoid communities with toxic positivity, judgmental behavior, or pressure to conform.

5. **Set personal goals for social interaction**
    - How often would you like to engage (daily, weekly)?
    - What do you hope to contribute and receive from the community?
    - Identify the boundaries you want to maintain while engaging.
6. **Identify healthy environments where you thrive**
    - Do you prefer structured groups with clear rules or informal peer support?
    - Consider whether you feel safer in person or online.
7. **Track your experiences**
    - After each engagement, reflect:
    - Did I feel supported or drained?
    - Did I leave feeling heard, valued, and respected?
    - Is this a space I want to return to?
8. **Review and refine your community list**
    - Periodically assess which groups feel valuable.
    - Don't be afraid to leave toxic spaces, even if they initially seemed helpful.
    - Prioritise communities that respect your boundaries and growth.
9. **Look for opportunities to give back**
    - Share your story if you feel comfortable - helping others can strengthen your sense of agency.
    - Offer support to newer members, helping create the safe space you wish you had found earlier.
10. **Celebrate your progress**
    - Building healthy community connections after experiencing manipulation or isolation is courageous.
    - Acknowledge every step you take toward rebuilding trust and finding your tribe.

By actively seeking out and participating in these supportive environments, you enhance your personal growth and contribute to a collective resilience that empowers everyone involved. In these spaces, you find allies in your journey, people who understand your struggles and celebrate your victories. You create a tapestry of support and understanding, one thread at a time.

Building Alliances for Emotional Protection

Navigating life's challenges, especially those involving manipulation, becomes significantly more manageable when you have a trusted alliance. These alliances act as anchors, offering emotional protection and a sense of resilience. See a small circle of individuals who understand your experiences, share your values, and support your emotional wellbeing. This trusted group becomes a cornerstone of strength, allowing you to lean on them during times of need and offering the same support in return. Each member brings unique insights and experiences, enriching the group's collective wisdom. Partnering with mentors within this alliance can provide invaluable guidance and perspective. Mentors, often having navigated similar challenges, offer advice and support, helping you to see situations from different angles. This partnership fosters a deeper understanding of manipulation and equips you with strategies to counteract it effectively.

Fostering mutual support within these alliances requires a commitment to reciprocity and shared responsibility. Regular check-ins with alliance members can be instrumental in maintaining emotional wellbeing. These interactions provide a platform for open communication, where members can express concerns, celebrate successes, and offer encouragement. Establishing group norms prioritizing confidentiality and respect is crucial for creating a safe space where members feel comfortable sharing personal experiences. These norms ensure that all interactions remain supportive and constructive, reinforcing the trust that forms the alliance's foundation. By fostering an environment where each member feels valued and heard, the alliance becomes a powerful tool for collective growth and resilience.

Incorporating diverse perspectives within your alliance can enhance understanding and problem-solving capabilities. Inviting members from different cultural backgrounds enriches discussions, offering varied viewpoints that challenge assumptions and broaden horizons. This diversity fosters a more comprehensive understanding of manipulation, highlighting how cultural nuances can influence behaviors and perceptions. Encouraging open dialogue about varied experiences with manipulation allows members to learn from each other's stories, gaining insights into how manipulation can manifest and how to counteract it effectively. These discussions promote empathy and understanding, strengthening the bonds within the alliance and empowering each member with new knowledge and strategies.

Maintaining healthy dynamics within your alliances is essential for ensuring their long-term sustainability and effectiveness. Setting clear boundaries and expectations for alliance interactions helps prevent misunderstandings and conflicts. These boundaries define the framework within which members operate, ensuring that all interactions remain respectful and productive. Utilizing conflict resolution techniques to address disagreements is vital for preserving the group's harmony. By approaching conflicts with a willingness to listen and understand, members can resolve issues constructively, maintaining the integrity of the alliance. Rotating leadership roles within the group can also promote equal participation and investment. This practice ensures that all members have the opportunity to contribute and take responsibility, fostering a sense of ownership and accountability within the alliance. By maintaining these healthy dynamics, alliances remain resilient and effective in providing emotional protection and support.

The power of alliances lies in their ability to offer strength, resilience, and a sense of belonging. These connections buffer against manipulation, ensuring you have a support network to rely on when facing challenges. Through mutual support, diverse perspectives, and healthy dynamics, alliances become a vital resource for personal growth and emotional protection. As you build and nurture these relationships, you create a foundation of strength that equips you to navigate the complexities of life with confidence and resilience.

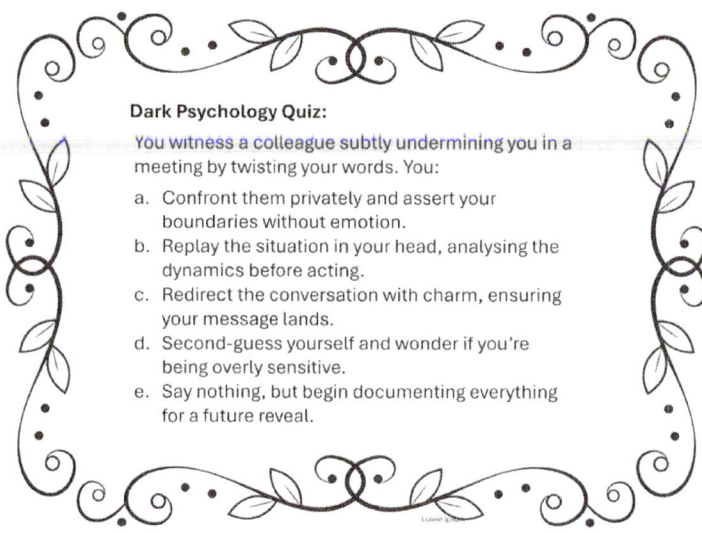

Dark Psychology Quiz:

You witness a colleague subtly undermining you in a meeting by twisting your words. You:

a. Confront them privately and assert your boundaries without emotion.
b. Replay the situation in your head, analysing the dynamics before acting.
c. Redirect the conversation with charm, ensuring your message lands.
d. Second-guess yourself and wonder if you're being overly sensitive.
e. Say nothing, but begin documenting everything for a future reveal.

Chapter 21: Continuous Growth and Learning

Adopting a growth mindset can transform your personal and professional life, helping you navigate an ever-evolving world confidently. Embracing lifelong learning sharpens your skills and instills a sense of purpose, enhancing your overall wellbeing as you uncover passions you never knew you had.

To effectively harness the benefits of lifelong learning, setting specific and achievable learning goals becomes crucial. The SMART criteria - Specific, Measurable, Achievable, Relevant, and Time-bound - offer a structured approach to goal-setting, ensuring clarity and focus. For instance, set a short-term goal to complete an online course within a month, enhancing your professional development. A long-term goal could involve mastering a new language over a year and broadening your cultural horizons and communication skills. By clearly defining your objectives, you create a roadmap for growth, motivating yourself to stay on track and celebrate your progress along the way. This approach boosts your confidence and empowers you to tackle challenges strategically.

Exploring diverse learning methods allows you to tailor your educational journey to your unique preferences and lifestyle. Online courses and webinars offer flexibility, enabling you to learn quickly and fit education into your busy schedule. For those who absorb information audibly, podcasts and audiobooks provide a rich source of knowledge during daily commutes or household chores. Meanwhile, workshops and seminars offer hands-on experiences, fostering interaction and engagement that deepen your understanding. By embracing various learning formats, you enrich your experience, discover new interests, and enhance your ability to adapt to different situations, all while maintaining balance in your daily life.

Despite the allure of lifelong learning, barriers like time constraints or lack of motivation can hinder progress. Implementing time management techniques, such as setting aside specific hours for study or integrating learning into daily routines, can help overcome these challenges. Creating a supportive learning environment at home, free from distractions, fosters focus and encourages consistency. Surrounding yourself with resources, like inspiring books or online communities, keeps motivation high and connects you with others on similar paths. Addressing these barriers with strategic solutions will pave the way for uninterrupted learning and sustained personal development, empowering you to achieve goals and unlock new potential.

In today's fast-paced world, staying informed is crucial for relevance and adaptability. Being aware of developments in your field ensures that you remain competitive and prepared for new opportunities. Subscribing to industry-specific newsletters offers steady updates while engaging with thought leaders on social media, broadening your perspective and exposing you to innovative ideas and discussions. These platforms provide invaluable insights and foster a sense of community among professionals. Yet, the sheer volume of information can be overwhelming. It's essential to filter information for quality and evaluate sources for credibility and bias. Cultivating a habit of inquiry and curiosity further enhances your understanding. Participating in Q&A forums like Quora or attending lectures and panel discussions can spark new interests and deepen your knowledge. Balancing information consumption with critical thinking and reflection is key. Setting designated times for reading and practicing digital detoxes can prevent burnout and enhance comprehension, ensuring that you remain informed without becoming overwhelmed.

Tools for Self-Assessment

Whether through personality quizzes like the Enneagram or Big Five, which reveal your core traits and how they influence your interactions, skills assessments that pinpoint your professional fortes, or emotional intelligence tests that delve into your social aptitude, these tools provide a comprehensive understanding of your landscape. They empower you to align your growth with your true self, guiding you toward more fulfilling personal and professional endeavors.

Incorporating feedback from peers and mentors enhances the clarity and depth of your self-assessment journey. Constructive feedback provides a lens through which you can view your actions and decisions from different perspectives. To gather such feedback, engage in open conversations with those you trust, ask for specific examples, and approach these discussions with an open mind. Reflect on your feedback, identifying recurring themes and areas ripe for development. This practice helps refine your self-perception and highlights hidden growth opportunities. By incorporating these external insights, you gain a well-rounded understanding of your capabilities and potential, setting the stage for informed and impactful goal setting.

Using self-assessment results to guide your goal-setting process ensures that your aspirations are grounded in reality. This alignment helps in setting realistic and impactful personal and professional goals. Reflect on your strengths and weaknesses, and craft goals that build on your existing skills while addressing areas for improvement. Regularly track your progress, celebrate achievements, and adjust plans as needed. This iterative process keeps your goals relevant and attainable, motivating you to strive for excellence. By consistently revisiting and refining your objectives, you focus on your growth trajectory, empowering yourself to achieve your fullest potential.

Engaging with online communities presents opportunities for personal growth, allowing you to connect with professionals and enthusiasts who share your interests. These platforms offer a rich tapestry of collaboration and knowledge-sharing, whereby diverse perspectives fuel creativity and innovation. Networking with individuals across various fields broadens your horizons and opens doors to new ideas and potential collaborations. By immersing yourself in these communities, you can access a wealth of information and support that significantly enhances your learning.

Finding the right online communities is essential to ensure alignment with your interests and goals. Begin by researching community values and engagement levels, ensuring they resonate with your aspirations. Platforms like Reddit, LinkedIn, or Facebook Groups serve as gateways to connect with like-minded individuals, each offering unique environments for discussion and exchange. Look for active groups where members contribute regularly and foster a positive, supportive atmosphere. This proactive approach helps you become part of a network that nurtures growth and shared understanding.

Contributing meaningfully, and not negatively, to community dialogue is vital for enriching both your experience and that of others. Start discussions on topics that interest you, inviting members to share their insights and perspectives. Respond thoughtfully to contributions, providing feedback and encouragement that fosters a collaborative spirit. By actively engaging in conversations, you demonstrate your commitment to the community, building a reputation as a valuable participant. This interaction enhances your knowledge and strengthens your connection to the community, creating a sense of belonging and mutual support.

Building meaningful connections within online communities involves more than just participating in discussions. Engage in virtual meet-ups or webinars to interact with members in real-time, deepening friendships and professional relationships. Collaborate on community projects or initiatives, combining skills and resources to achieve common goals. These activities foster a sense of camaraderie and create lasting bonds that extend beyond digital interactions. By nurturing these relationships, you develop a support network that encourages personal development and celebrates collective achievements.

Personal journaling is a powerful tool for emotional clarity, providing a safe space to process thoughts and experiences. The act of writing can significantly reduce stress and anxiety, offering a therapeutic release of pent-up emotions. By translating feelings into words, you enhance your emotional intelligence and self-awareness, gaining insights into your emotional patterns and triggers. Engaging with your innermost thoughts on paper can illuminate the path to self-discovery, helping you navigate complex feelings with greater ease and understanding. This practice is not just an exercise in reflection but a profound method to connect with your authentic self, fostering a deep sense of inner peace and clarity.

Exploring different journaling techniques can help tailor this process to your specific needs. Stream-of-consciousness writing allows for unstructured exploration, letting thoughts flow freely without the constraints of grammar or punctuation. This liberating approach encourages raw self-expression and uncovers subconscious ideas. Bullet journaling offers organization and planning, combining creativity with practicality to track habits, set goals, and organize thoughts systematically. For those seeking guided introspection, prompts provide focused reflection on specific themes or emotions, encouraging deeper contemplation of personal experiences. Each method offers unique benefits, catering to diverse preferences and facilitating a personalized journaling expertise that aligns with your emotional and cognitive goals.

Incorporating journaling into your daily routine ensures consistency and maximizes its benefits. Set aside dedicated time each day, whether in the morning to set intentions or in the evening to reflect on your day. Creating a conducive environment for reflection - quiet, comfortable, and free from distractions - enhances the quality of your journaling sessions. Whether you prefer writing in a cozy corner with a cup of tea or in a tranquil spot outdoors, find a space that inspires introspection and creativity. Regular practice transforms journaling from a sporadic activity into a meaningful habit, fostering ongoing emotional clarity and personal growth.

Journaling also serves as an effective tool for tracking progress toward personal goals. You maintain a written record of growth and milestones by reflecting on your achievements weekly or monthly. This practice not only celebrates your accomplishments but also identifies areas for improvement, guiding your future efforts. Visualizing future aspirations and outlining actionable steps within your journal creates a tangible roadmap for success. This process reinforces commitment to your goals, providing motivation and accountability. As you review past entries, you gain perspective on your journey, recognizing patterns and insights that inform your ongoing development.

Reflecting on past experiences with newfound insights can profoundly enhance your understanding and foster growth. Learning from mistakes and triumphs allows you to gain perspective on your personal development over time. Analyzing these moments uncovers patterns and themes that illuminate your journey. Techniques like creating timelines of significant events and writing reflective essays help draw meaningful lessons from your past. These exercises provide clarity and highlight how far you've come.

Applying insights from your past to current challenges fosters resilience and adaptability, helping you confidently navigate life's complexities. By identifying recurring patterns, you can develop effective strategies to address similar issues in the future. This approach turns past experiences into valuable tools for problem-solving, promoting growth and transformation. Embrace change as a natural part of life, using your past as a foundation for future development. Set intentions for personal evolution and celebrate progress and milestones along the way.

Developing a Personal Plan

By defining clear objectives and desired outcomes, you gain a concrete understanding of what you aim to achieve. Break these objectives into actionable steps, assigning timelines to maintain momentum and prevent overwhelm. Identify essential resources and support systems to bolster your journey, ensuring you have the tools needed for success. Regularly monitor your progress, adjusting your plan to align with evolving goals and circumstances. Set aside time for self-evaluation, using feedback and results to refine strategies and enhance effectiveness. Cultivate a growth-oriented mindset, viewing your action plan not as a rigid structure but a dynamic tool for continuous development. Embrace flexibility and openness, recognizing that new opportunities may arise unexpectedly. Celebrate achievements, use them as motivation, and learn from setbacks.

Reflective practices play a crucial role in fostering ongoing personal growth, serving as a guiding light that illuminates your path to self-awareness and insight. Regularly reflecting maintains a heightened awareness and intentionality in your actions and decisions. This process allows you to assess your experiences, extracting valuable lessons contributing to your development. Establishing a reflection routine, whether in the quiet calm of the morning or the tranquility of the evening, ensures consistency and impact. Incorporating mindfulness meditation as a tool for reflection enhances this practice, providing a serene space for introspection and clarity. Consider questions that prompt deeper understanding and growth as you delve into self-exploration. Contemplate what you've learned from your experiences today, how your beliefs and values have evolved, and what your current strengths and areas for improvement are. Through reflection, you can set personal and professional growth intentions, identify key focus areas for the coming months, and ensure balance and wellbeing in your life.

Change isn't inevitable; it's the lifeblood of growth and innovation. Adapting becomes crucial in our fast-paced world, where new technologies and ideas emerge daily. Embracing change allows you to stay relevant and seize opportunities others might miss. Consider how change acts as a catalyst for progress, pushing boundaries and challenging the status quo. By viewing change as an opportunity for growth, you unlock your potential and foster a mindset open to learning and innovation. This perspective transforms uncertainty from a source of fear into a realm of possibilities, encouraging you to seek out new experiences and embrace them wholeheartedly.

Building adaptability skills empowers you to navigate life's uncertainties with confidence and resilience. Flexibility in thinking allows you to approach problems from various angles, finding creative solutions that others might overlook. Cultivate open-mindedness to explore diverse perspectives, enriching your understanding of the world around you. Practicing curiosity keeps you engaged and motivated, eager to learn and adapt. Overcoming resistance to change requires confronting fears and limiting beliefs that hold you back. Identify and challenge these barriers, proving that growth lies on the other side of discomfort. Gradually expose yourself to new experiences, expanding your comfort zone and building confidence in your ability to handle change. Embrace change as a powerful tool for growth, setting goals that encourage continuous learning and adaptation. Celebrate each success and milestone, acknowledging your progress and reinforcing your commitment to personal and professional development.

Inspiring Stories of Transformation

Picture a woman laid off after years in a stagnant career. Instead of despair, she seizes the opportunity to transform her passion for painting into a thriving online art business. Her story is one of many that showcase how embracing change can lead to profound personal growth and fulfillment. Across various walks of life, individuals have faced adversity, whether through career upheaval or personal setbacks and emerged stronger by redefining their paths. These tales highlight the resilience and grit required to pivot toward a life of purpose.

From these stories, we learn the value of perseverance and the critical role of support networks. Mentors and peers often provide the encouragement needed to push forward. As you reflect on these narratives, consider your aspirations and how they align with your goals. Use these insights to set actionable steps, drawing from strategies others have successfully employed. Embrace challenges as opportunities for learning - and celebrate your milestones.

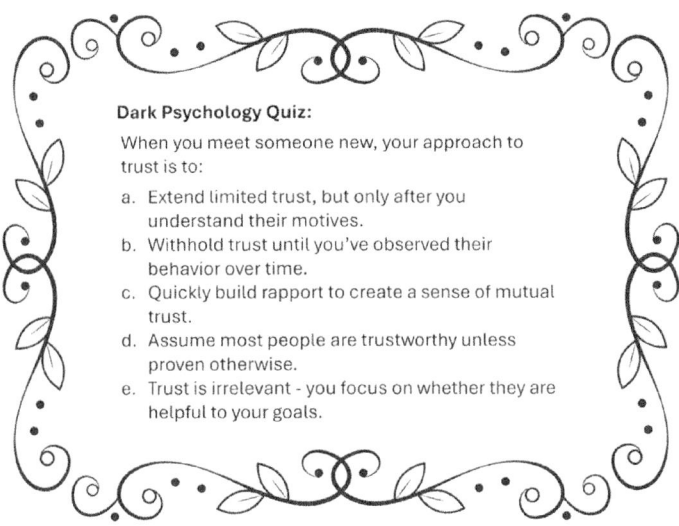

Dark Psychology Quiz:

When you meet someone new, your approach to trust is to:

a. Extend limited trust, but only after you understand their motives.
b. Withhold trust until you've observed their behavior over time.
c. Quickly build rapport to create a sense of mutual trust.
d. Assume most people are trustworthy unless proven otherwise.
e. Trust is irrelevant - you focus on whether they are helpful to your goals.

Takeaways

Throughout this journey into the depths of dark psychology and manipulation, we've uncovered the hidden forces that shape human behavior and influence. By delving into the foundations of persuasion, cognitive biases, and emotional manipulation, you've gained a deeper understanding of how these tactics can be used to control and exploit others.

From gaslighting and narcissistic abuse to the subtle art of deception, we've explored the common manipulation techniques that permeate our daily lives. You've learned to recognize the red flags of love bombing, guilt-tripping, and other forms of psychological warfare that can erode your sense of self and autonomy.

But this knowledge is not meant to instill fear or paranoia. Instead, it empowers you to protect yourself and those you care about from manipulation. By developing your emotional intelligence, setting clear boundaries, and cultivating resilience, you become the master of your destiny.

The insights you've gained from this book are theoretical concepts and practical tools for navigating the complexities of human interaction. From the workplace to your relationships, you now have the skills to recognize and resist manipulation in most forms.

But this is just the beginning of your journey. Personal growth and self-improvement are lifelong pursuits that require continuous learning and adaptation. By staying informed, reflecting on your experiences, and seeking out supportive communities, you can continue to build your emotional fortitude and thrive in the face of adversity.

Remember, the power of influence is a double-edged sword. While it can be used to deceive and control, it can also be harnessed for good. Using your knowledge ethically and responsibly can inspire positive change in yourself and others.

As you move forward, I encourage you to embrace the challenges ahead with courage and self-awareness. Draw strength from the lessons you've learned and the resilience you've cultivated. Know that you can shape your reality and create your desired life.

Through the power of storytelling, you, too, can rewrite your narrative. Whether you're an aspiring entrepreneur, a creative soul, or simply someone seeking to live authentically, the insights you've gained will serve you well.

So go forth confidently, armed with the knowledge and tools to navigate the complex tapestry of human behavior. You are the author of your own story, and with each chapter, you can grow, learn, and thrive.

The journey of self-discovery and personal empowerment never truly ends. Still, with the foundation you've built through this book, you are well-equipped to face whatever challenges lie ahead. Trust your inner strength, surround yourself with positive influences, and never stop learning.

As you continue to unravel the mysteries of the human psyche, know that you are not alone. The path may be winding, and the terrain uncertain at times, but with perseverance and a growth mindset, there is no limit to what you can achieve.

So, please take a deep breath, trust in yourself, and step forward into a future where you are the master of your own destiny. The power is within you, waiting to be unleashed. Embrace, harness, and let it guide you toward a life of authenticity, resilience, and boundless potential.

You've got this. Stay strong.

Psychological Profile Test: Which Archetype Are You?

How we respond to manipulation, persuasion, and power plays isn't random - our personality, experiences, and instincts shape it. Some people meet manipulation with their own quiet strategies, while others are more likely to charm their way out of trouble or confront it head-on. This psychological profile test is designed to help you uncover your default approach to influence and control.

You'll see a question at each chapter's end throughout this book. Each relates to the themes covered and asks how you would naturally react in certain situations. There are no right or wrong answers - just honest reflections of how you instinctively move through the world.

Once you've completed the test, you can tally your answers to reveal your dominant archetype. You may find yourself aligning firmly with one or seeing elements of two or more, which is entirely normal. This is not about boxing you into a label but instead giving you a better language to understand your strengths, vulnerabilities, and tendencies when navigating influence - both when you're using it and when it's being used on you.

It's important to remember that these archetypes are not fixed. You may shift between them depending on the context, your emotional state, or how safe you feel with those around you. Some people become more assertive after betrayal, while others retreat and become observers. This test is simply a snapshot of your current instincts - a mirror, not a judgement. By learning to recognise your patterns, you gain the power to choose your responses rather than be ruled by them.

Treat this as an exploration of your inner world. Knowing how you naturally respond is the first step in taking control of your narrative; no one else can do it for you. If you've not taken the quiz at the end of each chapter yet, please return and do so.

You'll have a total count for each letter you selected at the end of the psychological profile test. Each letter corresponds to a distinct psychological archetype designed to help you understand how you naturally respond to influence, manipulation, and power dynamics. There is no perfect score, and no archetype is inherently good or bad. Instead, each reflects a unique combination of traits, strengths, and vulnerabilities that shape how you navigate human interaction.

If you mainly selected 'a' answers, you align most closely with the fox archetype. The fox is a natural tactical persuader who instinctively looks for angles, motivations, and leverage points in any situation. Foxes are strategic thinkers, often several moves ahead of those around them. They are not necessarily manipulative for the sake of it, but they understand the power of subtle influence and know how to use it when needed. Their strength lies in their adaptability and quick thinking, but their tendency to overanalyze or assume everyone has hidden motives can lead to distrust or unnecessary conflict.

    You fall into the owl archetype if you selected mostly 'b' answers. Owls are highly perceptive observers and skilled at reading between the lines. They prefer to stay on the sidelines, gathering information and forming a clear picture before taking action. They value objectivity and self-control, making them resistant to emotional manipulation. However, owls can sometimes become overly detached, missing opportunities to assert themselves or form deeper connections because they prefer to watch rather than participate.

If you selected mostly 'c' answers, your profile fits the serpent archetype. The serpent is the natural charmer, someone who understands the power of charisma and uses it to build influence. Serpents excel at creating rapport and making others feel seen and understood, but they can also use their charm to distract or mislead. Their greatest strength is their ability to adapt to different social situations quickly. Still, they can also become dependent on external validation, sometimes blurring the line between authentic connection and manipulation.

If you mainly selected 'd' answers, you match the lamb archetype. The lamb represents the trusting soul, who tends to see the best in people and assume good intentions. Lambs value harmony and connection and are often generous with their time, trust, and emotional energy. This openness is a strength in healthy relationships, but it also makes lambs more vulnerable to manipulation, particularly by those who exploit their empathy. The lamb must learn to set firm boundaries to protect their emotional well-being without losing their kindness.

Finally, if you mainly selected 'e' answers, you embody the wolf archetype. The wolf is the mastermind, someone who sees manipulation as a tool to be used sparingly but with precision when necessary. Wolves are highly strategic and emotionally controlled, capable of playing the long game to achieve their goals. They are not easily influenced and often see through others' attempts at persuasion. However, this calculated mindset can make wolves appear cold or detached, and they must be careful not to isolate themselves from genuine connection in their pursuit of control.

Your dominant archetype offers insight into how you process influence, set boundaries, and engage with power dynamics. Some readers will find they match one archetype clearly, while others may notice traits from two or even three. This blending is normal, as no one fits neatly into a single category. The purpose of the profile is not to label you but to give you a framework for understanding your tendencies so you can recognize your strengths and your blind spots.

Armed with this self-knowledge, you will be better prepared to recognize manipulation, resist undue influence, and decide consciously how you want to interact with those who use dark psychology techniques. Whether you are naturally cautious like the owl or confident like the serpent, the goal is to become more aware of your patterns - and more capable of protecting yourself and others in the process.

Your archetype also offers clues about how you've adapted to your environment over time. Were you once overly trusting and learned to become more guarded? Have you developed charm or humour as a defence? These shifts tell a deeper story about your resilience and your evolving emotional toolkit. By reflecting on the events and relationships that shaped your responses, you begin to see your profile not as fixed, but as part of an ongoing narrative - one you have the power to rewrite.

As you move through this book and encounter various manipulation tactics, notice how your archetype might influence your reaction. Some may find themselves feeling energised by confrontation, while others freeze or withdraw. These tendencies aren't weaknesses, they're simply the starting point for growth. The more you understand your reactions, the easier it becomes to create intentional space between stimulus and response, which is where real power lies.

Ultimately, this isn't just about understanding how others influence you - it's about deciding what kind of influence you want to have in the world. Do you lead with empathy? With precision? With silence or assertion? Knowing your archetype helps you become a more conscious version of yourself - someone who not only navigates power dynamics wisely but also uses influence responsibly, without manipulation or coercion. That is the truest form of strength.

Thank You For Reading!

It's been a deeply personal project and I'm grateful you chose to spend time with it. Whether you're here to heal, protect yourself, or simply understand how influence really works - I hope these pages brought clarity, confidence, and something worth carrying forward.

I hope this book offers you not only insights, but a sense of strength. Whether you're here because you've been manipulated before, want to protect yourself in future, or you're simply curious about how power really works; I'm deeply grateful you chose to walk through these pages with me.

Stay curious. Stay conscious. You're more powerful than you've been led to believe - and more aware now than you were before.

If the themes in this book resonated with you, scan the QR code below to leave a quick review. It makes a huge difference for a small business owner like me - I very much appreciate any help you can give.

https://bit.ly/3TIaAgw

Stay strong.

Serena

Your Free Downloadable PDF Resources

Thanks to the amazing support from the backers during the *Dark Psychology & Manipulation* Kickstarter, we've created a full suite of powerful resources to help you spot, understand, and defend against manipulation.

Below you'll find all the digital downloads - designed to be practical, empowering, and easy to use. Whether you're building boundaries, recovering from toxic dynamics, or just getting clearer on your needs, these are for you.

Access your full resource bundle here:
https://www.turtletreepress.com/darkpsychresources
Password: str0ngb0undaries!

The full list of resources is below:

Main Digital Resources (Kickstarter Backer Rewards)

1. Red Flags PDF
   A practical illustrated guide to common manipulation tactics

2. Cheat Sheet PDF
   "How To Spot A Manipulator In 60 Seconds"

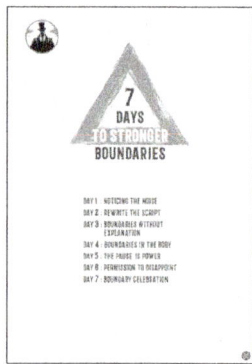

3. Defence Workbook PDF
   A deeper, interactive workbook

4. Mini Challenge
   7 Days to Stronger Boundaries
   Daily prompts, mindset shifts, and small actions

Secret Resource Vault (Unlocked Stretch Goals)

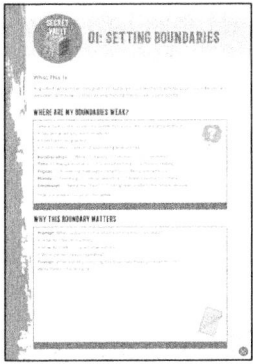 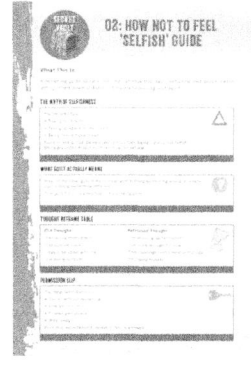

1. Setting Boundaries PDF
   A guided worksheet designed to help you understand where your boundaries are weakest, and how to start strengthening them clearly and kindly.

2. How Not to Feel 'Selfish' Guide
   A reframing guide to help shift the narrative that says protecting your peace means letting others down.

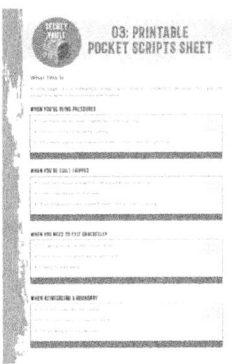 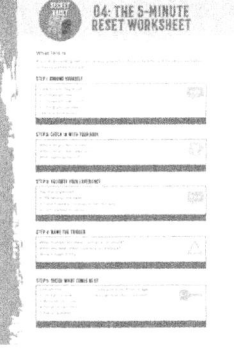

1. Printable Pocket Scripts Sheet
   A one-page quick-reference sheet with strong, respectful phrases for real-life situations where boundaries are tested.

2. The 5-Minute Reset Worksheet
   A quick, grounding exercise to help you return to clarity after a difficult conversation or manipulative moment.

Support Resources

Support Resources for Anxiety, Depression & Emotional Distress

If you're feeling emotionally overwhelmed, anxious, or low, know that you're not alone - and support is available. Below is a list of reputable organisations, platforms, and tools to help you navigate difficult mental health moments. These include helplines, therapy directories, online communities, and self-help resources.

Mental Health Helplines & Crisis Support

- Samaritans (UK): www.samaritans.org / Call 116 123 (24/7, free)
- Mind (UK): www.mind.org.uk / Mental health support and guidance
- NHS 111 (UK): www.111.nhs.uk / For urgent but non-life-threatening issues
- Shout (UK): Text SHOUT to 85258 / Free, confidential crisis text line
- Lifeline (US): 988 / www.988lifeline.org (24/7 national suicide prevention support)
- Crisis Text Line (US & Canada): Text HOME to 741741

Therapy & Professional Help

- BetterHelp: www.betterhelp.com / Online counselling and therapy access
- Talkspace: www.talkspace.com / Text and video therapy with licensed professionals
- BACP Therapist Directory (UK): www.bacp.co.uk / Find a qualified counsellor or psychotherapist
- Psychology Today: www.psychologytoday.com / International therapist search tool
- Mindler: www.mindler.co.uk / Online therapy sessions with licensed psychologists

Free Self-Help & Guided Tools

- MoodGym: www.moodgym.com.au / Cognitive behavioural therapy for anxiety & depression
- Headspace: www.headspace.com / Meditation and mindfulness app
- Calm: www.calm.com / Guided meditations and sleep support
- MindShift CBT App (Canada): Free app for managing anxiety
- NHS Every Mind Matters (UK): www.nhs.uk/every-mind-matters

Online Communities & Peer Support

- 7 Cups: www.7cups.com / Chat with trained listeners for free
- Elefriends (by Mind): Now part of Side by Side - supportive online community
- Reddit: r/mentalhealth, r/depression, r/anxiety - peer-led support (be mindful of content)
- Mental Health Forum: www.mentalhealthforum.net / UK-based online community

Emergency Help

If you or someone you know is in immediate danger, always call 999 (UK), 911 (US), or your local emergency services. Help is available - don't hesitate to reach out.

FUNDED ON
KICKSTARTER

THANK YOU

 TO ALL OUR BACKERS:

Andrea	Mickey	Shelley	Sophie	James Y.
Tenisha	Reyes	Hannah	Harley	Sasha
Aliya	Luke	Duncan	Kyle	Chris
Jereme	Geoff	Simon B.	Joe	Kaare
ThatStuart	Devid	Sarah	Blake	Kirsten
Marxorz	Jeff	Anthony	Curtis	Dave
Harald	Koby	Creamy	Ryan	Maggie
Giuseppe	Nancy	Matt L.	Oli	Chelly
Bryan	Matt J.	Richard B.	Nets	Brett
Ariel	Patrik	Christopher	Ty	James M.
Tony	Kenneth H.	Aaron	Lee	Matthias
Gunnar	Simon K.	Suzanne	Tom	Lorraine
Michael	Bradley	Max	Steve	Kenneth M.
Ravaka	Bettina	Alejandro	Edward	Stephanie
Corey	Renier	Paul	Melissa	Shirley
Jonathan	Angelique	Patrick	Emerald	Heather
Monica	Eileen	Abir	Richard R.	Caitlin
	Alex	Wes2733	Matthew	

Glossary

1. **Anchoring** - A cognitive bias where people rely heavily on the first piece of information they receive when making decisions.
2. **Authority Bias** - The tendency to attribute greater accuracy to the opinion of an authority figure and be more influenced by them.
3. **Bait-and-Switch** - A deceptive marketing or persuasion technique where someone is lured in with one offer but given a different, less desirable one.
4. **Bandwagon Effect** - The psychological tendency to adopt a belief or behavior because many others do the same.
5. **Behavioral Conditioning** - A process of learning through reward and punishment to modify behavior, often used in manipulation tactics.
6. **Brainwashing** - A coercive method of changing beliefs and attitudes through psychological manipulation.
7. **Breadcrumbing** - When someone gives minimal attention, affection, or communication to keep someone interested without committing.
8. **Catfishing** - A form of deception where someone pretends to be someone else online, often to manipulate or scam others.
9. **Charlatan** - A person who falsely claims to have special knowledge or skills, often manipulating others for personal gain.
10. **Coercive Control** - A pattern of ongoing intimidation, threats, humiliation, and isolation designed to dominate and control the victim's life.
11. **Cognitive Dissonance** - The mental discomfort experienced when holding conflicting beliefs or values, which manipulators exploit to influence decisions.
12. **Confirmation Bias** - The tendency to seek out or interpret information to confirm existing beliefs while ignoring contradictory evidence.
13. **Confirmation Conditioning** - When a manipulator rewards compliance and punishes resistance, training the victim to seek approval.
14. **Control Drama** - A term describing manipulative behaviors designed to gain attention, sympathy, or power in interactions.
15. **Covert Persuasion** - The act of subtly influencing someone's

thoughts or actions without them realizing it.
16. **Cult Mentality** - A psychological state in which a group exerts extreme control over its members, discouraging independent thought.
17. **DARVO** - An acronym for Deny, Attack, and Reverse Victim and Offender, a manipulation tactic used to shift blame.
18. **Dark Triad** - A psychological framework encompassing three personality traits: narcissism, Machiavellianism, and psychopathy.
19. **Deception** - The act of misleading or lying to someone for personal or strategic gain.
20. **Deflection** - A tactic used to avoid responsibility by shifting focus onto someone or something else.
21. **Discard Phase** - The stage in manipulative relationships where the abuser suddenly cuts off or devalues the victim after they've been used up.
22. **Dissociation** - A psychological state where a person detaches from reality, often as a defense mechanism against manipulation or trauma.
23. **Echo Chamber** - An environment where people are only exposed to information that reinforces their existing beliefs, limiting critical thinking.
24. **Emotional Addiction** - The cycle where someone becomes addicted to the highs and lows of a manipulative relationship.
25. **Emotional Blackmail** - A form of manipulation that exploits emotions like guilt and fear to control another person's behavior.
26. **Emotional Dumping** - Slightly different from trauma dumping - this is when someone unloads all their emotions onto another person without consent, creating an emotional imbalance.
27. **Emotional Withholding** - Deliberately withholding affection, praise, or emotional support to control someone.
28. **Emotional Manipulation** - Using psychological tactics to control or influence someone's emotions for personal gain.
29. **Emotional Transactioning** - The idea that every act of kindness comes with an unspoken debt, designed to make the victim feel perpetually obligated.
30. **Enmeshment** - A form of unhealthy relationship where boundaries are so blurred that the victim loses their sense of self, often seen in family dynamics.
31. **False Consensus Effect** - The tendency to overestimate

how much others agree with one's beliefs or behaviors.
32. **Fearmongering** - The deliberate use of fear to influence people's thoughts and decisions.
33. **Flying Monkeys** - People who a manipulator recruits to gaslight, pressure, or attack a victim on their behalf, often seen in narcissistic abuse.
34. **Framing** - A tactic where a manipulator spins events or conversations to fit a false narrative, painting themselves as the victim or hero.
35. **Future Faking** - A manipulative technique where someone makes false promises about the future to control another person.
36. **Gaslighting** - A psychological manipulation tactic that makes someone doubt their own perception and reality.
37. **Gaslighting by Proxy** - When a manipulator enlists other people to reinforce false narratives or question the victim's reality.
38. **Grandiosity** - An inflated sense of self-importance, often seen in narcissistic manipulators.
39. **Groupthink** - A phenomenon where a group prioritizes harmony over critical thinking, leading to irrational or unethical decisions.
40. **Halo Effect** - A cognitive bias where positive impressions of a person influence judgments about their other traits or actions.
41. **Hoovering** - A manipulation tactic where a toxic person tries to "suck" their victim back into a relationship after a period of distance.
42. **Hypnosis** - A trance-like state where a person becomes highly suggestible, sometimes used in manipulation.
43. **Identity Erosion** - The slow, intentional breakdown of a person's sense of self through constant criticism, gaslighting, and emotional manipulation.
44. **Illusory Truth Effect** - The tendency to believe false information after repeated exposure to it.
45. **Intermittent Reinforcement** - A manipulation tactic where rewards and punishments are given unpredictably to create emotional dependency.
46. **Isolation by Design** - When a manipulator systematically removes the victim from support systems like friends, family, or colleagues.
47. **Learned Helplessness** - A psychological condition in which

someone believes they are powerless to change their situation, often due to repeated manipulation.
48. **Love Bombing** - A tactic where someone overwhelms a person with excessive affection and attention to gain control over them.
49. **Machiavellianism** - A personality trait centered around manipulation, deception, and a lack of morality for personal gain.
50. **Manipulation** - The act of skillfully influencing or controlling someone's thoughts, emotions, or actions.
51. **Microaggressions** - Subtle, often indirect insults or dismissals, sometimes used intentionally to chip away at someone's confidence.
52. **Mirroring** - A subconscious or deliberate tactic where someone imitates another person's behavior to build trust and rapport.
53. **Misinformation** - False or misleading information spread intentionally or unintentionally to manipulate perceptions.
54. **Negging** - A manipulative tactic where someone gives backhanded compliments to lower another person's self-esteem and gain power over them.
55. **Neuro-Linguistic Programming (NLP)** - A psychological approach that suggests language and behavior patterns can influence people's thoughts and actions.
56. **Pathological Lying** - A chronic pattern of lying without a clear motive, often for control or self-preservation.
57. **Pavlovian Conditioning** - A learning process where repeated associations between stimuli shape behavior, often used in manipulation tactics.
58. **Persuasion** - The act of convincing someone to adopt a belief, attitude, or action, which can be ethical or manipulative.
59. **Planted Insecurity** - When a manipulator deliberately plants self-doubt in the victim's mind, even if no issue existed previously.
60. **Playing the Victim** - When manipulators portray themselves as the wronged party to gain sympathy and deflect blame.
61. **Projection** - A defense mechanism where someone attributes their negative behaviors or emotions onto another person.
62. **Psychological Warfare** - Using psychological tactics to destabilize or control an opponent.

63. **Reactive Abuse** - When a victim, after prolonged manipulation or provocation, explodes or acts out, allowing the manipulator to frame them as the abuser.
64. **Red Flag** - A warning sign that someone is manipulative, deceptive, or emotionally harmful.
65. **Reinforcement Loop** - A cycle where repeated behaviors and responses strengthen manipulation tactics over time.
66. **Shaming** - Using embarrassment, ridicule, or humiliation to manipulate someone into compliance.
67. **Silent Treatment** - Deliberately ignoring or excluding someone to punish or control them.
68. **Smear Campaign** - When a manipulator works to destroy the victim's reputation, spreading lies or half-truths to turn others against them.
69. **Stonewalling** - Refusing to engage in conversation, shutting down communication altogether to avoid accountability or to exert control.
70. **Subliminal Messaging** - Hidden or indirect messages that influence a person's thoughts or actions without conscious awareness.
71. **Toxic Positivity** - The insistence on only expressing positive emotions, even when it invalidates or dismisses real struggles - often used to silence complaints.
72. **Threat of Abandonment** - Using the fear of being left as a lever for control.
73. **Triangulated Trust** - When a manipulator sets themselves up as the only trustworthy source, severing the victim's connections to other perspectives.
74. **Triangulation** - A manipulation tactic where a third party is introduced into a conflict to create insecurity or competition.
75. **Trauma Bonding** - A psychological attachment that forms between a victim and their abuser due to cycles of abuse and affection.
76. **Trauma Dumping** - Oversharing deeply personal or traumatic experiences too early or in inappropriate settings, often to create premature intimacy or gain emotional control.
77. **Trust Erosion** - A slow breakdown of a person's confidence in their judgment due to prolonged manipulation.
78. **Victim Blaming** - A tactic where a manipulator shifts responsibility onto the victim, making them feel at fault for what has happened.
79. **Word Salad** - A form of verbal manipulation where a person

speaks in a confusing, circular, or nonsensical way to avoid accountability.
80. **Weaponized Guilt** - Twisting someone's natural sense of guilt into a tool to control their behavior.
81. **Weaponized Incompetence** - A tactic where someone pretends to be incapable of handling responsibilities to avoid doing them, shifting the burden onto others.
82. **Whistleblower Effect** - The phenomenon where exposing manipulation or unethical practices leads to backlash or retaliation.
83. **Wolf in Sheep's Clothing** - A metaphor for someone who appears kind or innocent but is actually manipulative or dangerous.
84. **Zeigarnik Effect** - A psychological principle that states people remember unfinished tasks or unresolved events more than completed ones, often used to keep people emotionally hooked in manipulative relationships.

More books by Serena Haywood:

http://www.turtletreepress.com

 @turtletreepress

 @turtletree_press

Explore more books from Turtle Tree Press:

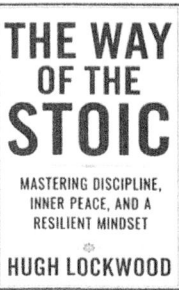

http://www.turtletreepress.com

 @turtletreepress

 @turtletree_press

Printed in Dunstable, United Kingdom